Unmothered By Black Mothers:
The Experiences of Black Daughters Who Are Detached from Their Black Mothers

Dr. Imani S. Steele

Published in the United States by Steele Compass LLC.

Steele Compass LLC
30 N Gould St #48693
Sheridan, WY, 82801

www.steelecompass.com

Cover design by Dr. Imani Steele Copyright © 2026 by Steele Compass. All rights reserved.

Cover design edited by The Art of Storytelling LLC.

Scripture quotations marked (AMP) are taken from the Amplified® Bible, Copyright © 1954, 1958, 1962, 1964, 1965, 1987, 2015 by The Lockman Foundation. Used by permission. www.Lockman.org

Scripture quotations marked (MSG) are taken from The Message, Copyright © 1993, 2002, 2018 by Eugene H. Peterson. Used by permission of NavPress. All rights reserved. Represented by Tyndale House Publishers, Inc.

Scripture quotations marked (NIV) are taken from the Holy Bible, New International Version®, NIV®, Copyright © 1973, 1978, 1984, 2011 by Biblica, Inc.™ Used by permission of Zondervan. All rights reserved worldwide. www.zondervan.com. The "NIV" and "New International Version" are trademarks registered in the United States Patent and Trademark Office by Biblica, Inc.™

All stories in this book, unless noted otherwise, are composites. Names have been changed to protect confidentiality.

The television series referenced throughout this work has served as more than cultural touchstones; they have been teachers. Grateful acknowledgment is made to the creators, writers, and producers whose storytelling made this analysis possible.

First edition: 2026

Trade paper ISBN: 979-8-9951550-0-3
E-book ISBN: 979-8-9951550-1-0
LCCN: 2026905895

To Black daughters who received less than what they deserved from their mothers. You're worthy of unconditional love. You're more than enough.

To my Mommy. Although you're not here, your story, our story, is embedded in this work. This is part of your legacy, so, with pride, I carry the baton you handed me. One day, we'll be together again, experiencing the fullness of what we both desired, with me as your daughter, and you as my mother. In the meantime, I have work to do. I'll see you soon.

Acknowledgments

First, to my doctoral committee, Dr. Piferi and Dr. Beiler, thank you for covering me during the process of conducting this research. Your grace and care set the tone for this study so that it could form into the beautiful masterpiece that God had always intended it to be. To the research participants, 17 beautiful, Black daughters who courageously shared their stories. Without you, this study, nor the book, would be possible. Thank you for trusting me with some of the most vulnerable parts of your story. To the village that raised me, words cannot express my gratitude for you all. I am the product of your prayers, love, and unwavering support. To the original Doctoral Daughters, thank you for being present. I will never forget the late nights, work sessions at Wegmans, moments of prayer, and our times of encouragement. It is a blessing to have amazing sisters on this journey with me. Last but certainly not least, now unto Him, who is able to keep me from falling, and present me faultless before the presence of His glory with exceeding joy, to the only wise God, my Savior, be glory and majesty, dominion and power, both now and forever. Amen.

Table of Contents

I What Was Never Said

1   I Wish I Had a TV Mom   7

2   The Sagacious Seventeen   24

3   The Evolution of Black Motherhood In America.   31

II The Weight of Her

4   Mothering That Wounded Daughters   42

5   How Detachment is Defined, Understood, & Lived   70

6   Relief & Rupture   92

III The Work of Becoming

7   Healing in Motion   108

8   Mothers Are Human, Too   127

9   Mothering to Break the Cycle   142

IV What God Says

10 The Dichotomy of Faith   160

V The Work That Remains for Us All

11 A Call to Action   180

Encouragement from the Sagacious Seventeen   197

A Letter to Black Daughters   203

Endnotes   205

I

What Was Never Said

1

I Wish I Had a TV Mom

Black Viewers & Meaning-Making

Research in media psychology demonstrates that viewers often form deep emotional attachments to television characters through processes known as parasocial relationships (PSRs) and identification.[1] These attachments become deeply felt relational experiences. When viewers identify with a character, they do more than observe a story unfolding on a screen. They enter it. The boundary between self and character softens. Viewers see through the character's eyes, feel their joy as relief, their disappointments as personal loss, and their struggles as intimately familiar.[2] This temporary merging of self and character creates an attachment that feels real, echoing the closeness, comfort, and even heartbreak found in relationships formed in everyday life. Therefore, PSRs offer more than entertainment. They foster connection, companionship, and a sense of belonging, shaping how we understand relationships, ourselves, and what care can look like.

For Black viewers, PSRs unfold within a cultural context shaped by long histories of misrepresentation, invisibility, and power imbalance.[3] Black audiences do not encounter media as passive spectators. Instead, they participate in it by actively interpreting, critiquing, and reworking media narratives through collective meaning-making. [4] Across platforms such as Black Twitter, Black Threads, and other digital spaces, Black viewers talk back to television. They discuss characters in real time, reframe story lines through cultural insight, and share emotional responses that extend far beyond the boundaries of the screen.[5] In many ways, these digital spaces function as contemporary extensions of the barber shop, the church, and the beauty salon, becoming virtual gathering places where Black people affirm shared identities, laugh together, grieve collectively, and care for one another.

The emotional weight of these PSRs becomes even clearer when situated within the historical landscape of Black women's representation in media. For generations, Black women on screen were reduced to rigid and dehumanizing stereotypes: the Mammy, the Sapphire, the Jezebel, the Matriarch, and the Welfare Queen.[6] As Patricia Hill Collins argues, these images were never neutral depictions. They functioned as ideological tools that justified Black women's subordination and hardship, normalized their exploitation, hypersexualized their bodies, and attempted to define Black motherhood itself.[7] The Mammy figure—depicted as content, asexual, and endlessly nurturing toward White families—was crafted to sanitize the violence of slavery by suggesting Black women found fulfillment in servitude.[8] The Sapphire stereotype framed Black mothers as loud, emasculating, and perpetually angry, shifting blame for structural inequities onto Black women themselves.[9] The Welfare Queen trope, popularized in the 1970s and continually resurrected in political discourse, casts Black mothers as irresponsible and morally deficient, positioning their children as social burdens rather than human lives.[10] These representations have consequences because they influence how Black girls and women are perceived and treated. Perhaps most critically, they create a representational void — a cultural absence where Black mothers who are emotionally available, nurturing, loving, and fully human are rarely visible. It is within this void that Black TV moms who resist these are admired by Black viewers. They are not simply characters. These women resist dominant narratives, affirming Black women's humanity and Black family life in contexts that have historically denied both.

Black TV Moms

Black TV shows have long been a site where Black daughters learn what motherhood can look like, sometimes more vividly than from their own homes. For many, Black TV moms were teachers, mirrors, and sometimes substitutes. Through them, viewers learned what tenderness could look like, what discipline sounded like, and what love felt like when it was expressed clearly or withheld entirely. Three Black TV moms in particular reveal the wide emotional range of Black motherhood: Clair Huxtable, Maya Pope, and Beth Pearson. Each represents a different way of mothering while Black, shaped by history, context, and their individuality. Together, they challenge the idea

that there is only one "right" way to be a good
Black mother and, by extension, only one kind of
Black daughter worth loving.

Clair Huxtable

Clair Huxtable from The Cosby Show is the
blueprint for Black motherhood. Not because she
was perfect, but because she was whole. Clair was
everything Black women were rarely allowed to be
on screen at the same time: a devoted mother, a
loving wife, and a successful attorney who did not
have to diminish herself to be palatable. She did
not sacrifice her career for motherhood, nor did she
outsource her presence at home. She managed her
priorities in a way that felt almost radical to some,
and inspirational for many. What made Clair so
powerful was not just what she did, but how she
did it. She loved each of her children uniquely,
without favoritism or emotional withdrawal. She
disciplined without humiliation. She corrected
without violence. In the now-iconic episode where
Vanessa is confronted for sneaking away to
Baltimore for "big fun," Clair delivers one of the
most formative lessons in Black TV history:
authority does not require harm.[11] Her voice is firm,
her boundaries are clear, and her love is never in
question. For many Black daughters, that scene
marked the first time they saw discipline modeled
without fear. It quietly suggested a truth that had
never been taught in countless Black households:
Love and correction can coexist without leaving
scars.

Clair Huxtable became the mother many Black
daughters wished they had been raised by or

hoped to become. She represented possibility. She helped Black daughters imagine a mother who was fully herself. She was a vision of Black motherhood untouched by chaos, where protection did not come at the cost of emotional safety.

Maya Pope from Scandal, by contrast, represents complexity.

Maya Pope

Maya is not the mother you aspire to emulate. She is the mother you are trying to understand. Absent for much of Olivia Pope's life — largely because she was hidden away by her ex-husband, Rowan Pope, a man who claimed to know what was best — Maya enters the story already positioned as the problem. She appears to be volatile, angry, and unpredictable. On the surface, she looks like the familiar Angry Black Woman trope, a dangerous mother, the one whose presence disrupts order. But that reading is shallow. Maya's frustration is history speaking. It is what happens when a Black woman's labor, loyalty, and sacrifice are endlessly demanded and never protected. Her now-famous "Admirable or Ridiculous?" monologue is not just directed at Rowan, a Black man who controlled and imprisoned her.[12] It is an indictment of a system that teaches Black women to save everyone else while abandoning themselves. Maya gives language to a truth many Black women know but are rarely allowed to articulate: That holding everyone together can cost you everything.

As a mother, Maya does not offer softness in the ways Olivia expects or wants. Not because Maya could not extend it—although she has every reason not to—but that is not the kind of mothering Olivia needed. Maya wanted to be soft and nurturing, but she quickly realized that Olivia needed a particular kind of mothering, partially due to how her daughter was groomed by Rowan. Rowan was the father who socialized Olivia to excel in a racist and sexist society. Maya was the mother who spoke hard truths to Olivia about how she had let her political ambitions consume every fiber of her being, which made her no different than her father. Maya could not be gentle with Olivia because she was facing a father who was not gentle with her. Maya mothers through truth-telling. Through confrontation. Through protection that arrives sharp-edged and unapologetic. It occurs in the way she tells her daughter, "Girrrlll, if you don't sit your dramatic a** down", or curtly advises Olivia to "Let it go" as she is in pursuit of Rowan, and plainly says to her child, "You don't seem to have much laughter in your life."[13,14,15] This is Maya's version of love. It is fierce, unpolished, and deeply maternal in a way that only a Black mother can be.

What Maya Pope shows us is something uncomfortable but necessary: Every Black mother does not need to be a Clair Huxtable, and not every Black daughter needs a Clair Huxtable. Some daughters need a mother who can see through their armor, address their wounds, and challenge the narratives they have inherited. Maya represents the Black mothers whose bluntness shapes their parenting, often resulting in their love being perceived as harshness. This is not excusing the harm but contextualizing it. She is flawed, yes, but she is also protective, discerning, and willing to tell the truth when silence would be easier.

Beth Pearson from This Is Us offers a third vision, one rooted in intention.

Beth Pearson

Beth gives viewers something that had been largely absent from TV for years. She is a Black mother in a loving marriage to a Black man, raising Black daughters with care, curiosity, and emotional responsiveness. Beth is not mothering from survival, but fierce devotion. What makes Beth compelling is her adaptability. She does not parent from a fixed script. She learns her children—Tess, Annie, and Deja—and adjusts her approach based on who they are and what they need. She offers tenderness even though she did not consistently receive it from her own mother. In doing so, Beth embodies a generational shift: Black women choosing to parent differently without abandoning structure or self-respect. Through Beth, Black daughters see something quietly transformative. Black women who are trying to do better than previous generations, parent differently, more gently, and adapt as the times see fit. We also see Beth show up on screen as a wife in ways that we had not seen previously. Beth, a Black woman, is married to Randall, an emotional Black man who wears his heart on his sleeve. She does not exist to fix him, nor does she disappear into his needs. Instead, she creates space for healing, holds boundaries, and expects accountability. Beth models what Black marriage and motherhood can look like in modern times, where children are becoming more expressive, where Black men are more vocal about their mental health needs, and where Black daughters are intentional about mothering differently than previous generations.

Together, these three mothers tell a fuller story of Black motherhood than any single character could. Clair shows us what was possible. Maya shows us what was endured. Beth shows us what is being re-imagined. For Black daughters watching, these women became more than TV characters. They became reference points—proof that the pain we felt had context, and that the love we longed for could take many forms. They remind us that Black motherhood is not monolithic. Sometimes it is inspirational. Other times, it wounds even when that is not a mother's intention. Either way, there is something about the Black mothers we see on screen that resonates with Black viewers on a personal level, and the extent to which these moms influence Black daughters should not be taken lightly.

The Mothers We Wish We Had

It is within this context—of PSR collective meaning-making, and the symbolic weight that Black TV mothers carry—that I asked the Black daughters in this study a seemingly simple question as an icebreaker: "If you could choose any TV mom to have raised you, who would it be and why?"[16]

The TV moms they named were women who embodied what attachment theory describes as secure and responsive caregiving, mothers who were consistently present, emotionally attuned, and nurturing. Their choices were not arbitrary. Each selection illuminated specific deficits in their own maternal relationships and revealed what these daughters understood healthy motherhood to require. Most daughters chose Clair Huxtable, whom they referred to as the model for Black motherhood. Michelle said:

"She was that girl! She's funny, she's fabulous, she's accomplished… she's stern, but she always circles back with love and compassion. She's the epitome of Black motherhood."[17]

Other daughters praised Mrs. Huxtable's ability to balance work and family life, noting that she was accomplished and still prioritized being a present mother and wife. The original Aunt Viv from The Fresh Prince of Bel-Air was the second most popular choice. Nia expressed:

"Aunt Viv was present, hands-on, and comforting. She showed all motherly aspects… in all ways, verbally and physically. She was a present mother to all of her children, and even those who weren't.[18]

Although most daughters mentioned Black TV moms, not all of them did. Hope shared why she chose Rebecca Pearson from This Is Us:

"She was willing to go to bat for her kids. Mothering is a very selfless job that doesn't come with a handbook. You have to be willing to put forth the effort and learn from the good and bad… lead by example and apologize to your children.

And I think that Rebecca shows her children that she's not perfect."[19]

The diversity of these choices — from Clair's professional competence and maternal warmth to Aunt Viv's nurturing expansiveness to Rebecca's willingness to repair — reveals something essential. These daughters were not fantasizing about perfection. They referred to emotional attunement. They desired a mom who had the capacity to correct without crushing. They wanted a mother who had the ability to love unconditionally. When discussing their preferred TV moms, they were describing mothers who loved and cared for their children with intention. The daughters in this study did not have that, and we're going to examine what happens when you do not.

A Translation of Academic Research

The findings and insights in this book are grounded in qualitative research that explored the lived experiences of adult Black daughters who are detached from their Black mothers.[20] The study explored how daughters described their experiences of detachment, the personal and cultural meanings they ascribed to it, and its impact on their lives. The study was guided by three research questions:

RQ1: How did Black adult women who have strained relationships with their Black mothers describe their lived experience of detaching from them?

RQ2: How did Black adult women describe what it means to detach from their Black mothers?

RQ3: How did Black adult women describe how detaching from their Black mothers impacts them?

The size of this study was guided by qualitative research standards suggesting that saturation—the point at which new data no longer produces new insight—is typically achieved with 9–17 participants.[21] Within this range, seventeen Black daughters shared their stories. Their participation was not simply a matter of meeting methodological criteria; it reflected a willingness to give voice to experiences often carried in silence.

Participants were recruited through social media platforms and selected after confirming they met the study's parameters. For this research, daughters had to identify as Black American, cisgender women, be at least 25 years old, and be detached from their biological Black American mothers who were still living, indicated by a minimum score of 18 on McCollum's Emotional Cutoff Scale (ECS) maternal sub-scale.[22] Each daughter participated in a 60-to-90-minute semi-structured interview conducted via videoconferencing. During these conversations, they recounted memories, named wounds, and reflected on the relationships that shaped their sense of self. Their narratives were analyzed using Braun and Clarke's thematic analysis approach, allowing patterns of shared experience to emerge across individual stories.[23]

Research on maternal detachment rarely centers Black daughters' experiences.[24] Bowen Family

Systems Theory (BFST), which provides the theoretical foundation for understanding detachment, conceptualizes it as a process where individuals manage unresolved attachment or emotional tension with family members by reducing physical and emotional contact. [25] Bowen theorized that detachment, while providing temporary relief from anxiety, does not resolve underlying relational dysfunction and often perpetuates patterns across generations.[26] While BFST offers valuable insights into family dynamics, it has seldom been applied to Black families in ways that account for the cultural, historical, and structural forces shaping Black mother-daughter relationships. This study addresses that gap. It centers the lived experiences of Black daughters who have made the deliberate, often agonizing decision to detach from their mothers, not out of disrespect or a failure to appreciate what their mothers endured, but out of necessity. These daughters have navigated the tension between cultural expectations of unwavering family loyalty and the need to protect themselves from relationships that were costing them their peace, their mental health, and their sense of self.

What This Book Offers

This book translates doctoral research into accessible scholarship that honors both academic rigor and the lived realities of the women who shared their stories. It speaks to multiple audiences, reflection, and understanding across different communities.

For Black daughters navigating strained or non-existent maternal relationships, this book offers validation, language, and framework. It articulates experiences that have often been unspeakable within Black communities. It affirms that you are not alone, not broken, and not betraying your culture by prioritizing your well-being.

For Black mothers, this book offers a mirror. Not one of accusation, but of reflection. The daughters in this study did not detach impulsively or without reason. Their decisions were rooted in years, often decades, of unmet needs, emotional harm, and relational patterns that made closeness untenable. For mothers willing to look honestly at their own behavior and its impact, this book provides insight into what daughters need and what happens when they do not receive it.

For therapists, counselors, and mental health professionals, this book offers cultural and theoretical grounding for supporting Black women navigating maternal detachment. It demonstrates how detachment functions differently in Black families, where expectations of loyalty, respectability, and familial duty intersect with racialized gender socialization and intergenerational trauma. It calls for therapeutic approaches that neither pathologize detachment as dysfunction nor romanticize reconciliation as the only path to healing.

For pastors, ministry leaders, and faith communities, this book examines the painful tension between biblical mandates to honor parents and the lived reality of daughters harmed by their mothers. It explores what honor looks like when a relationship is unsafe, how forgiveness can coexist with boundaries, and how the church can support healing without demanding that daughters return to harm.

For community organizations and social service providers, this book highlights the structural factors — economic marginalization, single motherhood, and lack of mental health support — that contribute to survival-based parenting and relational strain in Black families. It points toward preventive interventions that support maternal mental health and healing, potentially reducing intergenerational transmission of trauma.

The study that frames this book is grounded in qualitative phenomenological methodology, an approach designed to explore how individuals make meaning of lived experiences.[28] Phenomenology does not seek to generalize findings to all Black daughters or to make causal claims. Instead, it aims to capture the essence of a particular experience, and in this case, maternal detachment described by those who have lived it. The daughters' voices are centered throughout this book because their narratives are the data. Their words, their interpretations, and their reflections are what illuminate the phenomenon under study.

It is important to state clearly what this book is not. This is not an exercise in mother-bashing or an attempt to demonize Black mothers. The mothers in these daughters' stories were themselves navigating challenging circumstances. Many were likely doing the best they could with the resources and emotional capacity they had, which was often limited. Understanding context, however, does not erase harm. Acknowledging systemic oppression does not mean daughters are required to absorb its consequences in the form of maternal abuse or neglect. This book holds both truths: Mothers have been constrained by forces beyond their control, and daughters have been harmed in ways that warrant acknowledgment and healing.

Additionally, this book is not prescriptive. It does not tell you whether to reconcile with your mother, maintain limited contact, or sever ties completely. Those are deeply personal decisions that only you can make, informed by your specific circumstances. Finally, this work is not a substitute for therapy. If you are navigating maternal detachment or processing childhood wounds, professional support from a therapist who understands both family systems and the cultural dynamics of Black families is invaluable. This book can accompany that work, but it cannot replace the individualized, relational healing that therapy provides.

A content consideration: This book discusses maternal abuse, neglect, and trauma in detail. Daughters in this study describe physical abuse, emotional abuse, sexual abuse perpetrated by others while mothers failed to protect, parentification, and profound emotional neglect. If these topics are triggering for you, please engage with this material in ways that honor your capacity and prioritize your well-being. Read in the company of a therapist or trusted support system. Take breaks. Return when you are ready.

On Language and Approach

Throughout this book, the term "detachment" is used rather than the clinical phrase "emotional cutoff". While the research is grounded in Bowen Family Systems Theory, which employs "emotional cutoff" as its technical term, "detachment" feels more accessible and less pathologizing (regarded as mentally or psychological abnormality or disease). It also allows for a broader interpretation of the phenomenon. Detachment can be emotional, physical, or both. It can be complete or partial. It is permanent or subject to change. What matters is that it represents a daughter's intentional decision to create distance from her mother for the sake of her own well-being.

The terms "Black" and "Black American" are used throughout to refer specifically to descendants of American slaves. This is a distinct cultural and historical identity, different from the broader African diaspora. All participants in this study identify as Black American women, and the cultural dynamics explored here are specific to that context. While Black daughters from other parts of the diaspora—Afro-Caribbean, African immigrant, Afro-Latina—may share some experiences, their cultural contexts differ in meaningful ways that this study does not address.

Beginning the Journey

During each conversation with the seventeen daughters, it was evident that they needed the space and time to reflect on and discuss their experiences. They were courageous enough to do so, navigating moments of silence, tears, and conversations that forced them to recall some of their most painful memories. But they showed up. They were present not solely for this research, but also for the community. They all understood the importance of having this dialogue, and their willingness to be vulnerable in the service of collective healing is what makes this work possible. Their stories are shared with you now. Read them with the care and respect they deserve. Let them challenge you. Let them comfort you. Let them make you angry or sad or relieved or all of the above. If you see yourself in these pages, know that these seventeen women would want you to know: Your story matters too.

The TV moms these daughters wished for were not real. However, the kind of mothering they represented can be. Their love, presence, emotional safety, and unconditional acceptance. Black daughters deserve all of that. Not in a fictional living room, but in their real lives. This book examines why some daughters did not receive it, what happened when they did not, and how healing—individual, generational, and communal—becomes possible even in the absence of what should have been.

2

The Sagacious Seventeen

The Research Participants

The seventeen Black daughters whose stories inform this research are not abstractions. They are not case studies reduced to numbers or data points stripped of humanity. They are women with careers and callings, friendships and faith practices, dreams deferred and dreams pursued. They are daughters navigating the complex terrain of adulthood while carrying wounds from childhood. They are sisters, aunties, friends, sorors, godmothers, and in some cases, mothers themselves. When discourse references Black women who are educated, reflective, resilient, and committed to breaking cycles that have persisted for generations, they are discussing women like the Sagacious Seventeen. It's time for you to be introduced to these women in a way that establishes who they are, what they share, and why their experiences matter beyond their individual lives. These women represent a largely invisible population within Black communities: daughters who have made the deliberate decision to detach from their mothers not out of cruelty or caprice, but out of survival. Their stories were gathered so that daughters like them, and perhaps yourself, too, would no longer have to carry this experience without language, without validation, and without the knowledge that they are not alone.

Meeting the Sagacious Seventeen

These women are called the Sagacious Seventeen throughout this book, and that name was chosen deliberately. Sagacious means having good judgment, being perceptive, and demonstrating practical wisdom born from experience. Every woman in this study embodied that. They did not arrive at detachment impulsively or without reflection. They arrived there after years of discernment, learning from their mothers, reading patterns, adjusting expectations, and developing a clear-eyed understanding of what was and was not possible within their relationships. Many of them described how things looked immediately after detaching compared to where they stand now. The rawness of early detachment had, for most, given way to something steadier: A practical wisdom about their own lives and a realistic understanding of their mothers' limitations. Nobody in this study is living in delusion or denial. They have looked honestly at their circumstances and chosen to build their lives accordingly. That is sagacity. That is why they carry that name.

The daughters who participated in this study ranged in age from 27 to 49 years old, with a mean age of 35.12 years.[1] Their mothers ranged from 45 to 82 years old, with a mean age of 59.76 years. Generationally, the daughters included three Gen Z women, eleven Millennials, and three from Gen X; Their mothers spanned three generations: one from the Silent Generation, eight Baby Boomers, and eight from Generation X.[2] Eight of the seventeen daughters are mothers themselves, navigating the complex task of raising children while healing from their own maternal wounds. Participants were recruited from across the United States via social media platforms. Most were raised in the South Atlantic and Midwest regions, though they now reside primarily on the West Coast, in the Midwest, and in the South Atlantic parts of the United States. This geographic distribution reflects both the mobility common among educated Black women and, for some, the intentional creation of physical distance from their mothers.

Each daughter scored between 18 and 25 on the maternal subscale of McCollum's Emotional Cutoff Scale (ECS), with a mean score of 22.41.[3,4] These numbers represent more than statistical variation; they tell a story of distance deliberately created and carefully maintained. The ECS measures the degree to which individuals reduce emotional and physical contact with their mothers to manage unresolved attachment or relational tension.[5] The decision to set a minimum threshold of 18 (representing 72% of the maximum possible score) ensured that participants demonstrated moderate to high levels of maternal detachment rather than temporary distance or mild relational strain.[6] This threshold also distinguished everyday conflict from deep relational rupture, capturing experiences in which separation became a necessary strategy for daughters' well-being. The range of scores within the sample — from 18 to 25 — indicates variation in the intensity of detachment while confirming that all participants met criteria for significant maternal disconnection. Their experiences differed in degree, but they shared a common reality: Relationships marked distance, longing, and the complex weight of severed attachment.

Table 1: Descriptive Results

Participants	ECS Score	Generation	Age	Mom's Generation	Mom's Age	Age Mom Gave Birth	Kids(s)
Shandra	25	Gen X	49	Silent	82	33	Yes
Corrine	25	Millennial	42	Baby Boomer	62	21	Yes
Jen	22	Gen X	46	Baby Boomer	68	22	No
Diana	25	Millennial	39	Baby Boomer	66	27	Yes
Destiny	19	Millennial	33	Baby Boomer	63	30	Yes
Lisa	20	Millennial	38	Gen X	60	22	No
Charity	20	Gen Z	27	Gen X	45	18	No
Brooklyn	19	Millennial	29	Gen X	45	16	Yes
Michelle	25	Millennial	33	Gen X	55	22	Yes
Jasmine	22	Millennial	32	Baby Boomer	61	30	No
Amina	22	Millennial	32	Gen X	57	26	No
Nia	23	Millennial	31	Gen X	50	19	No
Joy	25	Gen X	45	Baby Boomer	74	29	No
Jada	24	Millennial	36	Gen X	57	21	Yes
Moesha	25	Millennial	42	Baby Boomer	64	22	No
Hope	22	Gen Z	27	Gen X	52	25	No
Mya	18	Gen Z	28	Gen X	55	27	Yes

What Table 1 cannot convey is the emotional weight each number carries. The ECS score of 25, the maximum possible, achieved by five participants, represents not only a measurement but the lived reality of completely severing contact after experiencing years of accumulated harm, which extinguished hope for reconciliation. The ages at which mothers gave birth, ranging from 16 to 33, hint at stories of teenage motherhood, unplanned pregnancies, and women becoming mothers before they had fully become themselves. Each pseudonym in that table represents a Black daughter who sat across from a computer screen and shared stories rarely, if ever, told in full. These women wanted other Black daughters to have language for their pain; they hoped this study would be the first of many to address this public health crisis in the Black community, and for many, it was finally time to tell their story.

Why These Stories Matter

These stories matter because they point toward the possibility of change. If we can understand what drives daughters to detach, then we can begin to interrupt those cycles. Change can occur, but it requires the willingness to look honestly at what has been happening inside Black families. The community also must resist the cultural reflex to protect the image of Black motherhood at the expense of the daughters it has sometimes failed. The seventeen Black daughters profiled in this chapter are not outliers. They are evidence of a pattern that Black communities have been reluctant to examine, and mainstream research overlooks.

When this study was announced on social media, hundreds of Black women responded with variations of the same messages:

"This is my story."

"Please keep me posted on the results!"

"Thank you for doing this work. This is what our community needs!"

The number of Black women who reached out to me, some to participate, others simply to express gratitude that someone was finally examining this experience, suggests that maternal detachment among Black daughters is far more common than cultural silence would indicate. These daughters' stories matter because they challenge the monolithic narrative of Black motherhood that dominates both popular culture and academic discourse. Black mothers are often portrayed—rightly, in many cases—as pillars of strength, as women who have mothered under impossible conditions and kept families intact against the odds.[8] That narrative is true and important. It is not the only truth, though. Some Black mothers have harmed their daughters, despite their best intentions or because of choices they made. Some Black daughters have been forced to choose between their mothers and their own well-being, and it is imperative to amplify their voices.

3

The Evolution of Black Motherhood in America

What Was Taken

Black motherhood in America was forged in the crucible of slavery, an institution that made traditional mothering impossible. Enslaved women had no legal claim to their children.[1] They could not protect them from being sold, from physical or sexual abuse, or from forced labor that damaged growing bodies and spirits. They could not decide where their children lived, what they ate, how they were raised, or whether they would be allowed to remain together as a family. Motherhood existed under constant threat.

The psychological violence of this reality cannot be overstated. Enslaved mothers lived with the ever-present knowledge that their children could be taken from them at any moment. Many endured the unbearable trauma of watching their children disappear into the domestic slave trade, never to be seen again. Under such conditions, some mothers chose to end their infants' lives rather than condemn them to a future in bondage — acts born not of cruelty, but of devastating and incomprehensible love to those outside the experience.[2] The trauma of forced separation produced a form of mothering shaped by the impossibility of attachment security, which poses a question: How does a mother allow herself to love fully when loss is inevitable?

Enslaved women also endured the painful contradiction of having to nurture their oppressors' children. They were forced to nurse, raise, and provide emotional care for White children while their own children were denied that same protection.[3] They performed the role of devoted caregivers within their masters' households while their own children were left in the care of elderly enslaved people, older siblings, or forced to fend for themselves. This dual reality — the woman who tenderly cares for White children while her own go neglected — was not a choice. It was a condition of survival. And it established a pattern that would echo across generations. Black women were trained to pour themselves into the care of others, rarely allowed to pour into their own homes. Thus, Black women became compelled to mother others before — or instead of — their own children.

After emancipation, the conditions that constrained Black motherhood did not disappear. They simply took new forms. During Reconstruction and the subsequent decades, many Black women worked as domestic servants in White households, a continuation of the labor they had performed under slavery, now for wages that barely sustained life.[4] These jobs demanded long hours and often required live-in arrangements, once again separating mothers from their children. Black women cared for White families while their own children were raised by grandmothers, aunts, or older siblings. Out of this reality emerged what scholars describe as "othermothering," a communal caregiving model that became essential to Black families' endurance.[5] When biological mothers could not be present, other women in the community stepped forward — grandmothers, aunts, neighbors, church mothers, and fictive kin who were family in every sense but blood. This collective approach to raising children was both a response to structural constraints and a cultural strength rooted in African traditions emphasizing shared responsibility and communal care.[6] The saying "it takes a village to raise a child" was not metaphorical in Black communities. It was a lived reality. For Black children whose mothers could not be present, the village sustained them. Concurrently, it also left some of them with a complicated relationship to the woman who gave birth to them but was rarely there. Those children learned early that mothers could not always be present, a lesson that quietly shaped their expectations of maternal love and availability. The communal care giving model also meant that "mothering" was diffused across multiple people, replicating patterns experienced by enslaved children — the absence of consistent maternal presence that leaves an emotional imprint that followed them into adulthood.

What slavery and its aftermath ultimately established was a model of Black motherhood shaped by absence, sometimes as the trade-off for provision. Black mothers were systematically put in a position where they could not tend to their own homes or children, whether by force or economic needs. From the onset of their existence in America,

Black mothers did not live in the conditions necessary to provide emotional attunement or sustained nurturing. These were not failures of individual mothers. They were adaptations to systems designed to make Black motherhood nearly impossible.

What Was Taught

If slavery made motherhood impossible, Jim Crow made it perilous. Black mothers during this era had to prepare their children not just for economic hardship but for physical danger. They had to teach their children how to navigate a world where a perceived slight to a White person could result in lynching, and where walking on the wrong side of the street or making eye contact could be fatal.[7] This was not abstract fear. This was a lived reality, reinforced by the photographs of Emmett Till's mutilated body, by stories of neighbors who disappeared, and by the ever-present threat of violence that required constant vigilance.

Black mothers during this era had to perform an impossible balancing act. They had to instill dignity while teaching submission, cultivate pride while rehearsing deference, and affirm their children's humanity while preparing them for a world determined to deny it. This process became what scholars now describe as racial socialization, a deliberate preparation to help children navigate racism through code-switching, emotional control, and behavioral self-monitoring.[8] For Black daughters in particular, this preparation took on a gendered dimension. Mothers taught them how to survive racism and sexism as Black women living in a society that scrutinized and punished their bodies and voices differently. What we now understand as gendered racial socialization emerged from this point in history; daughters were taught how to be Black and how to be female in a world that threatened them for both.[9]

These lessons were not matters of preference. They were survival strategies. They required a form of mothering that prioritized compliance over expression and emotional control over authenticity. Black mothers could not afford to raise children who freely expressed anger or spoke their minds without caution, because such openness could place their children in danger. So, they taught restraint, silence, and self-surveillance. Respectability politics emerged as another layer of this strategy.[10] If Black families could demonstrate moral character, hard work, discipline, and refinement according to White middle-class standards, perhaps they could secure safety and dignity. Black mothers enforced these standards with particular intensity, closely monitoring their daughters' clothing, speech, and behavior.[11] These efforts were meant to shield daughters from racist stereotypes. They also constrained authenticity and self-expression. Daughters learned that they represented not only themselves but the entire race, and that any misstep could be used to justify continued oppression.

Black mothers also modeled a form of strength defined by emotional containment.[12] They showed their children how to endure without complaint, how to conceal fear, and how to persist despite pain. Within this context, the Strong Black Woman schema began to crystallize as both a cultural expectation and a protective strategy; although its roots trace back to slavery, it became an explicit socialization practice during Jim Crow and the Civil Rights era.[13] Black mothers taught their daughters to be strong because the world would not protect them. They taught them to be independent because depending on others was dangerous. They taught them to suppress vulnerability because showing weakness could be exploited.

What passed from mother to daughter across these decades was not simply a set of behaviors. It was an entire emotional framework: strength means silence, survival requires self-denial, and protection demands distance. These lessons helped generations of Black daughters navigate a hostile world. They also shaped how daughters understood care, safety, and love, and they influenced how those daughters, when they became mothers themselves, would raise their own children. But the problem is that daughters do not only need to be prepared for the world. They need to feel safe in their own homes, too. They need tenderness alongside strength. And for many Black mothers, shaped by generations of survival, tenderness had become a language they were never taught to speak.

What Was Inherited

The Sagacious Seventeen's mothers raised their daughters during a period that spanned from the

1970s to the early 2000s. By then, the Civil Rights Movement had opened doors that previous generations could not access. Yet these same decades introduced structural forces that destabilized Black communities and intensified pressure on Black families in ways that directly shaped the homes these daughters grew up in.

The Sagacious Seventeen's mothers did not begin parenting from a neutral place. They inherited scripts shaped by centuries of survival-based mothering, which emphasized strength, sacrifice, vigilance, and endurance. What changed in their generation was the specific forms of pressure they faced. Chief among them was the War on Drugs, a federal policy that began under Nixon and escalated dramatically under Reagan, whose consequences landed squarely in Black households.[14] Mandatory minimum sentencing laws established stark disparities that disproportionately targeted Black communities, resulting in the mass incarceration of Black men.[15] The removal of fathers, brothers, and partners from Black homes was not incidental. Rather, it was a structural outcome of policies calibrated to produce exactly that result. Black mothers were left to shoulder the full weight of caregiving alone, often under conditions of financial instability and social scrutiny.[16]

The welfare reform movement that followed compounded these pressures. The Reagan administration popularized the "Welfare Queen" narrative portraying Black mothers as irresponsible and exploitative of government aid.[17] Subsequent welfare reform dismantled safety nets that had allowed mothers to meet their children's basic needs, forcing Black women who were already facing discrimination in hiring into impossible choices between survival and stability.[18] Some policies even penalized the presence of male partners in the home, effectively incentivizing family separation.[19] The result, for many Black daughters in and outside of this study, was a childhood shaped by a mother who was stretched beyond her capacity: working multiple jobs, navigating single parenthood without adequate support, and parenting from a place of exhaustion that left little room for emotional attunement.

Layered on top of these structural pressures was something more insidious: the specific form of oppression Black women face at the intersection of racism and sexism, what scholars term misogynoir.[20] Black mothers navigating this era were simultaneously hyper-visible and invisible, scrutinized, stereotyped, and surveilled, yet denied full recognition of their humanity or need for care. The problem became cyclical. When Black women experience racism and sexism from multiple sources—White men and women, and even from Black men—their natural emotional responses to these injustices get pathologized and reframed as evidence that they are inherently "the Angry Black Woman", which undermines their credibility and compounds their isolation.[21] The psychological burden of surviving these conditions while raising children often produced exactly what daughters describe in this study: Mothers who were emotionally unavailable, chronically stressed, quick to anger, and unable to offer the warmth and consistency their daughters needed.

The important truth underneath all of this is that for many of the Sagacious Seventeen, their mothers were not simply difficult women. They were women who had inherited survival strategies from generations before them, emphasizing provision, endurance, and emotional suppression. Several of the daughters' mothers parented without adequate support, without healing their wounds, and often without any model of what tender, emotionally present mothering looked like. What landed in the Sagacious Seventeens' homes was the accumulated weight of all of that. And the daughters bore its impact.

Understanding Without Excusing

Black motherhood has a history that is both brutal and beautiful. Black mothers loved fiercely under conditions designed to make love impossible. They sacrificed endlessly to give their children what they themselves never had. They embodied strength because anything less would have meant their families' destruction. It is a history that commands both respect and grief.

It is also a history that explains, though it cannot excuse, why some Black mothers wounded their daughters. The emotional suppression that kept families safe from White violence also kept Black mothers and daughters from connecting emotionally. The emphasis on strength and independence that helped Black women endure also foreclosed vulnerability and interdependence.

The focus on material provision that ensured physical survival sometimes meant emotional needs went unmet. The trauma of living in a racist and oppressive society shaped how Black mothers parented, often in ways that wounded even as they protected.

Understanding this history does not require Black daughters to minimize their pain or forgive harm that has not been acknowledged or repaired. It does not absolve mothers of responsibility for how they parented. What it does is provide a framework for holding complexity. Black mothers were constrained by forces beyond their control, and Black daughters were harmed by their mothers' responses to those constraints. Both things are true. The daughters in this study are not naive about the conditions their mothers navigated. Many of them can articulate, with striking clarity, the historical and systemic factors that shaped their mothers' behavior. Some of them understand that their mothers were doing the best they could with what they had. Concurrently, understanding does not erase hurt, though. History provides context, but it does not heal wounds, and that is what we will discuss next.

II

The Weight of Her

4

Mothering That Wounded
Daughters

Naming What Happened

If you're a daughter who has a strained relationship with your mother, before you read what follows, I want you to consider that what you have carried quietly for years has a name. More than one, actually. And the Sagacious Seventeen have described terms precise enough to finally make the unnamed things visible. This chapter names the forms of harm the Sagacious Seventeen endured at the hands of the women who were meant to protect them, nurture them, and love them without condition. It gives language to experiences that are often minimized, misunderstood, or left unspoken. As you read their words, I invite you to listen for your own story in theirs. You may not find an exact match. You may see something similar—a dynamic you recognize, a feeling you have had but never been given language for—and that recognition is the point. For mothers reading this, I challenge you to consider whether the maternal behavior described reflects how you parented your daughters. These pages may trigger defensiveness, guilt, or grief. If they do, avoid burying those feelings because they indicate that there is something for you to address within yourself, and possibly with your own daughter. For those seeking to understand why some daughters detach from their mothers, these pages provide answers that are neither simple nor comfortable. It is precisely this complexity that makes amplifying Black daughters' voices so important.

This chapter responds directly to RQ1, which asks: How did Black adult women who have strained relationships with their Black mothers describe their lived experience of detaching from them? illuminating the lived experiences that shaped participants' decisions to detach from their mothers. What emerges is a portrait of detachment as a response to wounds that began in childhood and were often reopened through more recent interactions. These stories reveal how early relational injuries, when left unaddressed, do not remain in the past; they live on in adult relationships, shaping distance, boundaries, and the eventual decision to sever ties. What follows is not a comprehensive catalog of every way a mother can fail their daughters. Rather, it documents the patterns that emerged from interviews with the Sagacious Seventeen. Their stories make clear that detachment is not capricious. It is not the result of daughters being ungrateful, oversensitive, or insufficiently committed to family. It is the culmination of years—often decades—of relational harm. It is the result of unmet needs, repeated injuries, and the persistent absence of repair.

What the Sagacious Seventeen trusted me with, I now trust you with. Receive their stories with the care they deserve.

Maternal Absence: The Foundation of Disconnection

All seventeen daughters in this study described experiencing some form of maternal absence during their childhoods.[1] For some, this absence was physical. Their mothers were simply not there—missing from the rhythms of daily life, and absent from moments that shape a child's sense of safety and belonging. Care, guidance, and presence were withheld, sometimes by circumstance and sometimes by choice. For others, the absence was emotional. Their mothers were physically present but emotionally distant, unavailable, unresponsive, or unwilling to offer the attunement, comfort, and reassurance their daughters needed. These daughters lived alongside their mothers yet felt alone. Their pain went unnoticed, their emotional needs unmet, and their inner worlds unseen. Presence without connection became its own form of abandonment. Some daughters experienced both forms of absence simultaneously, growing up with mothers who were neither reliably present nor emotionally accessible when they were around. In these homes, daughters learned early that proximity did not guarantee care and that closeness did not ensure protection.

Maternal absence is perhaps the most fundamental wound described by participants because it was established early that mothers could not be depended upon. Attachment theory tells us that children require consistent, responsive caregiving to develop secure attachment—the foundational sense that the world is safe, that needs will be met, and that they are worthy of care.[2] Regardless of its form, when mothers are absent, daughters often learn the opposite lesson: that the world is unpredictable, that their needs will not be reliably met, and that survival depends on learning to function without the person who should be their primary source of security.

Physical Absence

Physical absence took various forms across participants' childhoods. For some daughters, mothers were absent due to work demands. Joy recalled her mother's career as a politician:

"My mom was the bigger politician, the one who was more in the public eye, always traveling. My mother never attended a single one of my soccer games or basketball games. She never supported me. She was not even present for my birthday until I turned 16 years old."[3]

Joy's experience illustrates how even when absence is tied to legitimate work obligations, daughters still experience the impact. Joy understood intellectually that her mother's career was demanding, but emotionally, she registered that her mother chose other priorities over being present for her daughter's life. Other daughters described mothers who were absent due to romantic relationships. Corrine discussed how her mother's involvement with various men created a pattern of instability:

"She would move out with her boyfriend and then move back in and move out. Floating in and out [of the house] while I stayed with my grandparents."[4]

The unpredictability of her mother's presence made it impossible for Corrine to develop a sense of security with her mom. Her mother's romantic life took precedence over her responsibility to provide stable caregiving. For daughters whose mothers were frequently absent, extended family members often stepped in to fill the gap. Brooklyn explained:

"I don't remember where my mom was too much… meals were prepared by my grandmother. My mom would help, sometimes, with homework, but when it came to school pickup and mostly everything else, it was my grandmother."[5]

The communal caregiving model that is common in Black families functioned as intended. Brooklyn's grandmother ensured she was fed, clothed, and educated. This arrangement also meant Brooklyn never developed a primary attachment to her mother. Her grandmother became the maternal figure, while her biological mother remained present occasionally but never reliably. The pattern of grandmothers raising daughters while mothers remained in the background appeared across several of the daughters' stories. Joy plainly stated:

"I was raised by my grandmother who stepped in."[6]

Diana recalled:

"My grandmother pretty much did most of the raising."[7]

Regardless of the specific reason for physical absence, the impact was the same: Daughters learned they could not count on, nor should expect their mothers to be present. This lesson, imprinted early and reinforced repeatedly, laid the groundwork for eventual detachment, begging the question: If a mother is not present during childhood, when dependence on her is developmentally appropriate and necessary, why would a daughter expect her to show up later?

Emotional Absence

Even more painful than physical absence for some daughters was emotional absence, having a mother who was physically present but emotionally inaccessible. These mothers provided materially, ensuring daughters had food, clothing, and shelter, but could not provide emotional attunement, validation, or comfort. Several daughters described relationships with their moms as "transactional" or "functional", rather than nurturing.[8] The relationship centered on meeting basic survival needs without attention to emotional or relational needs. Amina articulated this dynamic with striking clarity:

"There was no conversation about living life. It was all about just getting to the next day. There was never any, like, how was your day or like, how are you feeling? It was, did you die? Were you fed? Did you have clothes? Okay, end of discussion."[9]

Amina's description captures the essence of emotionally absent mothering. Her mother ensured physical survival but showed no interest in her feelings, her experiences, or her personhood beyond basic functioning. The relationship was reduced to a checklist: alive, fed, clothed. Anything beyond that fell outside the scope of what her mother considered necessary or appropriate. For daughters raised with this form of mothering, emotional needs went chronically unmet. Destiny mentioned:

"I didn't go without [physical things], but the attention I needed from my mom was not present."[10]

The distinction Destiny draws is crucial. She acknowledges that her mother provided materially. However, material provision without emotional presence leaves daughters feeling that their mothers see them as problems to be managed rather than people to be known and loved. Further, emotional absence often meant daughters had no one to turn to when they were hurting, confused, or in need of guidance. Shandra stated:

"I didn't have a mom that I could trust… that I could share things with, that I could tell things to. So, when I became a preteen and a teen and things were happening to me, I didn't have a safe person that I could go to."[11]

The absence of a safe person during adolescence—a developmental period when daughters particularly need maternal guidance around relationships, body changes, and identity formation—left Shandra vulnerable and isolated.[12] She could not confide in her mother about "things that were happening," suggesting experiences that required protection or support her mother was unable or unwilling to provide.

During my conversations with the Sagacious Seventeen, I learned to consider that there is a particular grief in being raised by someone physically present and still unreachable. It is the grief of proximity without intimacy because you are growing up alongside a person who could not see you, not because you were invisible, but because she was unavailable to look. Daughters raised with emotionally absent mothers may struggle to name this as a wound precisely because their mothers were technically there. The lights were on. The bills were paid. But their emotional needs were not met.

The Wound of Absence

Whether physical, emotional, or both, maternal absence communicated to daughters that they were not worthy of their mothers' time or attention. These messages shaped daughters' core beliefs about themselves, leaving them to question if they were worth showing up for. Maternal absence also taught daughters that they could not depend on anyone, that asking for help was futile, and that emotional self-sufficiency was the only viable strategy. Several daughters described becoming hyper-independent as children, learning to meet their own needs because waiting for their mothers meant those needs would go unmet indefinitely. This adaptation served them in some ways — they became resilient, resourceful, capable — but it also foreclosed the possibility of healthy interdependence in relationships. If you learn at age seven that you cannot depend on your mother, that lesson shapes every relationship that follows.[13] The foundation of maternal absence created the groundwork for detachment. These daughters learned young that their mothers would not show up. That lesson, once learned, is difficult to unlearn.

Maternal Abuse: Harm Inflicted by the One Who Should Protect

Twelve out of seventeen daughters gave accounts of being physically and emotionally abused by their mothers during childhood.[14] The abuse took multiple forms. Maternal abuse is particularly devastating because it represents a betrayal of the most fundamental relationship. Mothers are supposed to be protectors. They are supposed to be safe. When the person whose role is to shield you from harm is the source of harm, it creates a psychological bind that is difficult to escape. Where do you go for safety when the person who should provide it is the threat?

Physical, Verbal, & Mental Abuse

The physical abuse daughters described ranged from what might be culturally normalized as "discipline" to violence that was clearly excessive and dangerous. Shandra succinctly summarized her mother's behavior:

"She was verbally abusive. She was emotionally abusive. She was physically abusive."[15]

The matter-of-fact way Shandra listed these forms of abuse — as if cataloging known facts rather than describing trauma — suggests how normalized the abuse had become. It was simply her reality. Nia described psychological abuse, inflicted with disturbing intention:

"I pretty much was mentally and emotionally tormented growing up. My mom would say, 'I am gonna play with your head. You're going to be my emotional punching bag,' all the time."[16]

This is not accidental harm. This is an act of a mother deliberately targeting a child as a receptacle for adult pain, revealing a level of cruelty that is difficult to comprehend. Some daughters described mothers whose abuse manifested as relentless bullying. Moesha wrote a poem about her mother that captures the emotional quality of this dynamic:

"Cold, callous, cruel, and controlling. Vile, vicious, and vain. Hurtful. Not helpful. Mean girl, a bully. I just called it a different name — Mom."[17]

The language Moesha uses reframes maternal abuse in terms typically reserved for peer relationships. But recognizing her mother as a bully allowed Moesha to name what was happening: she was being targeted, belittled, and emotionally terrorized by the person who should have been her primary source of support.

Parentification and Adultification

Parentification and adultification, the processes by which children are forced to take on responsibilities inappropriate for their developmental stage, were common forms of emotional abuse that daughters experienced.[18] When mothers abdicated their caregiving responsibilities, most of the daughters were expected to fill the gap. This meant raising younger siblings, managing household tasks, providing emotional support to mothers, and in some cases, functioning as the primary decision-maker in the family. Amina described the role reversal she experienced:

"It was always her running to me for help, me helping her out of situations, giving her life advice… But it's never really been reciprocated on my end."[19]

This role reversal robbed Amina of the opportunity to be a child, to receive guidance rather than constantly provide it. Brooklyn shared her experience of being responsible for her younger sister's care and education:

"When we were not in my grandmother's house, I had to take care of my little sister. Help her with homework, take her to school, and make sure she eats. I was very much involved in my little sister's education. I was [the main one] talking to teachers during [parent-teacher] conferences."[20]

Moesha's experience of parentification was even more extreme:

"I felt like a single mother. I was the mother. I was the one who found babysitting. I packed the bottles. I put the kids to sleep… studying for my AP calculus test with a baby on my chest, trying to rock him to sleep."[21]

The image of Moesha studying for calculus with a baby on her chest encapsulates the impossibility of her situation. She was being asked to do what no child should have to do: be both child and adult and a student and mother, all at once.

The long-term impact of parentification and adultification is well-documented in psychological literature. Children who are forced into adult roles prematurely often struggle with boundary-setting, have difficulty accepting help, and carry resentment toward the parents who abdicated responsibility.[22] For the daughters in this study, parentification also created a fundamental confusion about what the mother-daughter relationship should be. Spending your childhood taking care of your mother's emotional needs or raising your siblings can make you question what it means to be a daughter. Where is the space for them to receive care rather than constantly provide it? Furthermore, the harm of parentification is not always visible in the way that physical abuse is visible. It leaves no marks. It can even look, from the outside, like a capable, mature child. However, it teaches a daughter to suppress her own needs so thoroughly that she sometimes cannot locate them at all. She can become a woman who defaults to giving because receiving feels foreign, even dangerous. She may find herself dismissing her own needs before anyone else has a chance to meet them. This is not a character flaw, but an unfortunate byproduct of parentification and adultification.

Failure to Protect

Perhaps the most painful form of maternal abuse described by participants was not direct harm but failure to protect daughters from harm perpetrated by others. Four daughters shared stories of being physically or sexually abused by paternal figures or male family members, and in each case, their mothers failed to intervene.

Jen described an incident in which her father attacked her when she was eleven years old:

"My father attacked and tried to murder me [when I was 11 years old]. When I explained what happened to [my mother], she went, "What did you do?' She was very much complicit in the abuse. Not only did she not stop it, but she would also often place the blame on me."[23]

Jen's mother's response shifts responsibility from the adult perpetrator to the child victim. Rather than protecting her daughter or holding her husband accountable, Jen's mother blamed Jen for provoking the attack. This response compounds the trauma of the initial abuse by communicating that Jen is not worthy of protection, that her father's violence is somehow her fault, and that her mother will not be a source of safety. Nia also shared a similar experience of disclosure, met with disbelief and disgust:

"There were instances where I told her what my stepdad did to me. She looked me in my face with disgust, and she said, 'No. Oh my God, you can't be serious.' I never felt comfortable coming to her for anything [after that]."[24]

Nia's mother's refusal to believe her, along with the disgust with which she responded, is a betrayal that likely inflicted as much harm as the abuse itself. When a child discloses abuse and is not believed, the message is clear: Your reality doesn't matter, your safety doesn't matter, and the adult you're accusing is more important than you are.

Diana's experience occurred within the context of religious abuse that her mother not only enabled but also fell victim to:

"We were both being trafficked in the name of the Lord at the cult my mother brought us to..."[25]

Diana and her mother were both being victimized within a cult, but her mother's allegiance to the cult leader meant she could not protect her daughter.

These accounts of maternal failure to protect reveal a devastating truth. Some daughters learned that their mothers would not choose them, even when choosing them meant protecting them from violence. This lesson, that you cannot depend on your mother to keep you safe from harm, creates a wound that persists long after the abuse ends. It suggests that you are on your own because no one will intervene on your behalf, and your worth is insufficient to warrant protection.

What these daughters trusted to their mothers — their safety, their pain, their disclosure of harm done by others — their mothers could not receive. And what is perhaps most important to hold here is that the pain of not being protected is not the same as the wound of the original harm. The pain deepens when you reach for your mother and find her aligned with, or not defending against, the very thing that wounded you. For daughters who have experienced this, they question why they were not protected. They also wonder something quieter and more devastating: Why did my mommy not choose me?

Harsh Treatment: Criticism, Perfectionism, and Conditional Love

Even among daughters who were not explicitly abused, harsh treatment characterized by relentless criticism, impossible standards, and conditional acceptance created its own form of wounding. These mothers communicated — through their words, tone, and actions — that their daughters were never enough. No achievement warranted praise. No effort satisfied. Daughters lived under constant scrutiny, aware that love and approval were contingent on performance. For many, their mothers were their first critics. Rather than encountering the world's harshness outside the home and finding refuge within it, these daughters experienced the home itself as a site of emotional injury. The person tasked with protecting their self-worth instead became the primary source of its erosion.

Unrelenting Criticism and Impossible Standards

Several daughters described mothers who focused relentlessly on what was wrong rather than what was right. Michelle explained:

"My mother had very, very high standards...
left me feeling that I was never good enough. I
could do my best effort, and my mother would find
three different ways I could have done it better."[26]

The moving target of "good enough" is
devastating. If excellence is never sufficient, and if
every achievement is met with identification of its
flaws, daughters internalize the message that they
are fundamentally inadequate. Daughters, like
Michelle, could never rest in their accomplishments
because their mothers would immediately redirect
attention to what was missing. This pattern of
criticism often began early and persisted across
daughters' childhoods and into adulthood. For
instance, Mya described her mother's explicit
parenting philosophy:

"My mom would say, 'I don't want you to think
that you're perfect. I'm always going to tell you
when you're wrong. I'm not going to build you up
too much. I'm going to make fun of you.'"[27]

Mya's mother articulated her belief that building
up her daughter would somehow harm her, that
humility required constant deflation. But what Mya
experienced was not healthy humility. It was a
chronic undermining of her worth.

Attacks on Appearance and Identity

For some daughters, maternal criticism centered
specifically on their physical appearance. Moesha
recalled:

"[My mom] would say, 'You dark, you fat, you
Black. Look at your big calves, your big thighs.'

And you know, that was definitely something that scarred me. I used to think I was the ugliest… mind you, my mom is dark-skinned."[28]

Moesha's mother's comments — attacking her for being dark-skinned, using "Black" as an insult — reflect internalized anti-Blackness that gets transmitted from mother to daughter. Rather than helping Moesha develop pride in her appearance and identity as a Black woman, her mother taught her to see her Blackness as something shameful. The lasting impact is evident in Moesha's statement, as her mother's words used to shape her entire self-concept. Other daughters described mothers who attacked their emotional expression. Destiny stated:

"When it came to me expressing my emotions or my feelings, I was crazy. I was Sybil. I was too deep. I was evil."[29]

Destiny's mother critiqued her daughter's emotions, using labels like "crazy" and "Sybil" (a reference to a woman with dissociative identity disorder) to dismiss and invalidate Destiny's feelings. The message was clear to Destiny: Your feelings and thoughts are not just unimportant; they are evidence of something wrong with you.

Daughters as Outlets for Mothers' Pain

A particularly distressing dynamic described by multiple participants was the sense that their mothers used them as outlets for unresolved pain related to other people or circumstances. Mothers who resented their own lives, their romantic lives, or their circumstances directed that resentment at their daughters. Corrine explained how her mother's anger about an unwanted pregnancy shaped their entire relationship:

"She absolutely hates me. She's made it clear that she hates me. She's never wanted me from conception. She never wanted me. She was forced to have me because my grandfather didn't believe in abortion and wouldn't give her money for an abortion."[30]

Being told you were never wanted — from conception forward — creates a foundational sense of being a burden, of taking up space you have no right to occupy. Jen described a similar dynamic, in which she and her siblings became visible evidence of their mother's resentment and disappointment:

"[My siblings and I] were the reasons why she couldn't live the life that she wanted. So, we're living, breathing manifestations of her own oppression. Like little scarlet letters."[31]

Other daughters discussed how they took the brunt of their mothers' anger due to the failed romantic relationships that they had with their fathers. Hope shared:

"She would say, 'Oh, you're just like your father', … ma'am, you decided to have a baby with him. I knew she was trying to insult me because she could not insult him. She would call me names, but she was actually trying to express how she felt about him."[32]

Nia experienced this same dynamic:

"My mom is absolutely triggered by me because I look like my dad. I remind her of my dad… I told her that on the phone one day during an argument, and she went silent. She didn't deny it, she didn't agree, but she absolutely went silent, which, to me, spoke volumes."[33]

These accounts reveal how some mothers used their daughters as emotional dumping grounds, repositories for rage, disappointment, and grief that had nothing to do with the daughters themselves. Daughters became reminders, and in some instances, triggers, of their mothers' constrained choices, failed relationships, or thwarted dreams.

The dynamics that shaped daughters' early experiences with their mothers laid the foundation for patterns that continued to unfold over time. The emotional burdens placed on them, the lack of nurture, and the absence of safe connection did not simply fade as daughters grew older. Instead, these early wounds became the blueprint for ongoing interactions. As daughters moved into adolescence and adulthood, many hoped for change — for growth, accountability, or emotional maturity from their mothers. What they encountered instead was the painful realization that the same relational patterns persisted, setting the stage for the lack of mothering they would continue to experience later in life.

Emotional Immaturity and Unavailability in Adulthood

What ultimately moved many participants from enduring to detaching was the painful recognition that the patterns that wounded them in childhood did not remain in the past. They persisted. As daughters entered adolescence and adulthood, their mothers did not change or develop the capacity to engage differently as their daughters matured. Instead, they continued to demonstrate the same emotional immaturity and unavailability, replicating in new contexts the same behaviors that had wounded their daughters as children.

Inability to Accept Accountability

Sixteen out of seventeen daughters indicated that their mothers respond with defensiveness or dismissiveness when confronted about past or present harm. Mothers could not tolerate honest conversation about their impact. They could not apologize authentically. They could not sit with their daughters' pain without making it about themselves.

Jen described her mother's typical response to being held accountable:

"I've told my mother on multiple occasions that she failed as a parent. And she still makes it about her… It [becomes] about her own situation. She's never going to accept responsibility or take accountability."[34]

Jada described a different but equally problematic response—mothers who resort to self-deprecation when confronted. She mentioned:

"[My siblings and I] are always trying to reassure her that we don't hate her when we bring up things from the past."[35]

An encounter such as this makes it impossible to address hurt because doing so requires managing the mother's emotional fragility. Then, some daughters discussed how their mothers' apologies are performative rather than genuine. Hope explained:

"My mother apologizes like the students I used to teach in 3rd grade. I stole your pencil. I'm sorry you feel that way."[36]

The inability of mothers to accept accountability meant that repair was impossible. Daughters could not heal within the relationship because their mothers would not acknowledge the wounds they had inflicted. This pattern of defensiveness, deflection, and self-pity wore daughters down over time. Eventually, many reached a point where they stopped trying to have honest conversations because doing so only resulted in further hurt.

Mothers Remaining Unavailable

The transactional nature of these relationships that formed during the daughters' upbringing extended into adulthood for many participants. Lisa explained how even during a medical emergency, her mother's focus remained on what

Lisa could do for her rather than on Lisa's well-being:

"I was in the ER and was still paying her bills. And she was calling me about something. I told her I was in the ER. She was like, 'Well, don't forget to pay my light bill.' She doesn't have much sympathy for me, but she expects it from me."[37]

Lisa's experience demonstrates how emotional absence is not solely about when mothers fail to provide sympathy or concern but also consists of the one-directional nature of the relationship. Daughters are expected to show up for their mothers while receiving little reciprocal care. Charity described a similar pattern of one-sided engagement:

"For the last six to seven years, she'll call me, or I'll call her just to check in on her, and she will talk for one hour or an hour and thirty minutes, and then we get off. I share very little. [She doesn't] provide space or time for the conversation to be about me."[38]

The inability or unwillingness of Charity's mother to make space for her daughter's life reveals emotional self-absorption that forecloses genuine relationships because, in this instance, when contact occurs, it centers entirely on the mother's needs, leaving the daughter invisible.

Perhaps the most heart-wrenching evidence of mothers' ongoing emotional unavailability emerged in daughters' stories of mothers failing to show up during moments of acute vulnerability.

These are moments when daughters most needed maternal support, and these are the moments when many mothers were coldest, most dismissive, or simply absent. Michelle shared her experience of miscarriage:

"I also had a miscarriage before I got pregnant with my daughter, and my mom didn't give me the response that I needed. She was cold. I very vividly remember her threatening to have me deemed incompetent because I wasn't happy. And when I told her, 'Well, most women get six weeks after they have a child before they're expected to return to normal. And I lost two children in a matter of three weeks,' her response was, 'So you need six weeks?'"[39]

Joy described her mother's response to stillbirth:

"My mom had to make the decision [to keep either my daughter or me alive] because I was not married. She decided to save her daughter. So, my daughter was stillborn. My mother does not acknowledge or speak about my child because she's one of those people who is out of sight, out of mind."[40]

These experiences of their mothers' self-centeredness and coldness during daughters' most vulnerable moments confirmed what daughters had learned in childhood: their mothers could not be counted on for emotional support.

The Mother Wound

Collectively, the mothering during childhood and ongoing emotional immaturity described created what clinicians often refer to as the "mother wound", an often unconscious injury that shapes how daughters see themselves, navigate relationships, and understand their own worth based on the unmet needs, neglect, and dysfunction they experienced with their mothers.[41] The mother wound often manifests in beliefs daughters formed about themselves based on how they were mothered. For instance, if your mother is absent, you may learn that you are not important enough to warrant presence. If your mother criticizes you relentlessly, it is possible you believe you are fundamentally flawed. If your mother cannot see you, you think that you are invisible. These lessons get encoded at a level that precedes language and logic, becoming part of how daughters perceive themselves and experience the world.[42]

Several daughters described feeling fundamentally unlovable. If your own mother — whose care should be the most certain thing in the world — does not love you well, what does that say about your worthiness of love? Corrine articulated this sentiment in her certainty that her mother hates her. Moesha captured it in her mother's belief that she was ugly. These are not minor insecurities. These are core beliefs about the self, shaped by maternal messages absorbed over a lifetime. Moreover, the mother wound manifests in relational patterns. Daughters who grew up unable to trust their mothers often struggle to trust anyone.[43] The self-sufficiency daughters developed is an adaptive response. It kept them safe when depending on their mother was dangerous, but this response can also limit capacity for intimacy and interdependence in relationships that might actually be safe. Lastly, the mother wound shapes daughters' emotional lives as well.[44] Many described struggling with perfectionism, people-pleasing, or chronic feelings of inadequacy. These are all attempts to earn the love and approval they never received from their mothers. Others described emotional numbness or difficulty accessing feelings, having learned early that emotions were unacceptable or dangerous.

The mother wound is not a metaphor. It is a documented, legitimate psychological injury that shapes the architecture of a daughter's inner life. It lives in the beliefs she holds about her lovability, in the relationships she gravitates toward, in the standards she holds herself to, and in the way she responds when she is needed by others or when she needs something herself. If you recognize yourself in what has been described here — the perfectionism, the difficulty trusting, the persistent sense that you are somehow not enough — those responses were not born in you. They were learned. They are rational adaptations to an environment that asks you to survive without adequate support.

The Process of Detaching

For the Sagacious Seventeen, detachment was rarely triggered by a single incident. It unfolded slowly, almost imperceptibly at first, developing over time through an accumulation of experiences that left daughters accustomed to disappointment, emotional and physical exhaustion, disregard, and the persistent feeling of being unloved by the very person who was supposed to nurture them. Detachment was not an impulsive withdrawal. It was a process that began with recognition. At some point in adulthood, daughters came to understand that their mothers were not willing, or not capable, of changing. This realization did not emerge suddenly. It surfaced gradually, shaped by years of repeated interactions that followed the same painful pattern. Each conversation that ended in dismissal. Each attempt at repair that was denied. Each moment of vulnerability met with indifference, hostility, or silence. Over time, hope eroded.

This accumulation of hurt is difficult for outsiders to grasp. From the outside, a single incident may appear minor, forgivable, or manageable. But for these daughters, no moment existed in isolation. What others might perceive as a small disagreement or misunderstanding was experienced as the latest entry in a long history of wounds, another confirmation of what they had learned repeatedly since childhood: this mother could not or would not show up differently. Detachment, then, emerged not from one event but from the cumulative weight of thousands. Within this gradual process, many daughters described what they understood as a last straw moment, an incident that crystallized what they had long been feeling and knowing. These moments varied in severity, but they shared a common function: They made the continuation of the relationship, in its existing form, emotionally or physically unsustainable.

For some, the turning point came when they recognized that their mothers were unwilling to protect them. Joy described an incident with her brother:

"[My brother got mad at something] I said or did, and lunged and almost hit me. My mom… by not speaking up for me, she defended him. And I was like, seriously, all the things I've done [for you], and you can't even come to my defense at all. Like you just let this happen."[45]

For others, verbal degradation was the straw that broke the camel's back. Mya recounted:

"I was on the phone with [my mom]. She called me out for not saying hi to her boyfriend. I was like, 'Girl, I have much bigger issues in my life going on than saying hello to this man.' She ended that call with, 'F*ck you, little b*tch,' and hung up."[46]

For Diana, she recognized the futility of staying connected to her mother, and that her decision to detach was tied to her own survival:

"I left the cult my mother brought us to [after 20 years]. It was pure hell. The manipulation of the cult leader. [To her], he was a prophet, you know? Direct connection to God. Total sociopath."[47]

Even if daughters did not describe a last straw moment, they referenced a turning point when the futility of hoping for change became undeniable. They had nothing left to give. The reserves they had drawn on for years — patience, hope, willingness to try again — were depleted. Daughters described feeling as though continuing to engage with their mothers would require them to sacrifice their own well-being in ways they could no longer afford. For several daughters, the turning point involved accepting that they could not change their mothers; they could only adjust how they responded. Destiny spoke about the futility of trying to get her mother to understand her:

"I spent years hoping and waiting for [my mom to understand me], and it's only broken me every time. It is what it is. I know what I can and cannot share with her. [Now], our conversations are surface level."[48]

Hope also articulated:

"I can't change people. I have to just change how I react to it."[49]

Eventually, the Sagacious Seventeen stopped expecting their mothers to be the maternal figures they deserved and adjusted their expectations accordingly. Daughters stopped investing energy in hoping their mothers would transform and started focusing on how to guard themselves from continued harm. Once daughters accepted their mothers' limited capacity, they could stop waiting for something different and start making choices based on reality rather than hope.

5

How Detachment is Defined, Understood, & Lived

Beyond the Dictionary Definition

Understanding how detachment happened does not fully capture what detachment meant to the daughters who chose it. This is where we turn to RQ2, which asks: What meaning did Black adult daughters ascribe to their detachment from their mothers? Moving beyond causes and catalysts, this chapter centers on daughters' interpretations of their experiences — the emotional, cultural, and psychological significance of choosing distance. What emerged from their accounts was clear: detachment is not a single, fixed experience with a universally agreed-upon definition. It is deeply personal, emotionally layered, culturally embedded, and practically complex. For some daughters, detachment represented freedom. For others, it was a loss. For many, it was both at once. The meanings daughters assigned to detachment were profoundly shaped by cultural context. The daughters are detached within communities that prize family loyalty, elevate motherhood as sacred, and often interpret separation from one's mother as betrayal rather than survival. Within these cultural frameworks, choosing distance is not simply a relational decision; it can be perceived as a moral and social rupture, one that carries consequences

70

for how daughters see themselves and how they are perceived by others.

To understand what detachment meant to these daughters requires holding multiple truths simultaneously. Detachment was necessary and painful. It was protective and grief-inducing. It was an act of self-preservation and a source of guilt. It offered relief while producing loss. It created space for healing while leaving behind unanswered questions and enduring longing. Most importantly, their stories reveal that Black daughters who detach are not navigating only individual relationships with their mothers. They are navigating entire systems of meaning—cultural expectations, communal values, and deeply rooted beliefs about motherhood, family, and obligation— that shape how their choices are understood, judged, and lived.

Personal Definition: What Detachment Means to Daughters

When asked "What does detachment mean to you personally?", the Sagacious Seventeen offered nuanced and reflective descriptions that revealed detachment to be far more complex than mere estrangement or avoidance.

Emotional Disconnection as Core Experience

For fifteen of the seventeen daughters, detachment was described primarily as an emotional state of disconnection rather than solely as the absence of physical contact. [1] This distinction is crucial. Daughters could be in the same room as their mothers, exchange pleasantries at family gatherings, fulfill caregiving obligations, and still be profoundly detached. The detachment was internal, a protective withdrawal of emotional investment and vulnerability. Some articulated why they made this as a conscious choice made in adulthood. Jen explained:

"My mother complained to me about my sister wanting advice for her first pregnancy. She said, 'I've raised my children, it's time to focus on me.' I started to become more and more separated because she made it clear where her line was. So, I gave her what she wanted. From the emotional and psychological standpoint, I've separated from her".[2]

Other daughters described never having felt emotionally connected to their mothers, even in childhood. Charity reflected:

"90% of the time she was my boss and 10% of the time she was my mom. And when she was being my mom, it was really only to discipline me. It wasn't necessarily to nurture me."[3]

For daughters like Charity, the maternal relationship has always been hierarchical and functional rather than emotionally intimate. This instance of detachment in adulthood simply formalized what had been true all along: Charity and her mother did not have an emotional bond. Jada shared a similar experience:

"We never had a close relationship. I cannot remember a time that we hugged or kissed or were just affectionate at all in our family."[4]

The absence of physical affection throughout Jada's childhood signaled a broader emotional disconnection. When she speaks of being detached from her mother now, she is not describing the loss of something she once had; She is naming the continuation of distance that has always characterized their relationship. This aspect of detachment meant that daughters could maintain some level of contact with their mothers while remaining emotionally separate. The relationship existed at a surface level without emotional vulnerability or intimacy.

Protection and Self-Preservation

Across participants' definitions, detachment was consistently framed as a necessary measure to safeguard mental health, emotional well-being, and overall stability. When asked what detachment meant personally, Shandra succinctly responded:

"Peace and protection."[5]

These two words encapsulate what many daughters expressed in longer terms. Detachment created space for them to experience safety and peace that was impossible while remaining closely connected to their mothers. Moesha's articulation of self-preservation was visceral:

"You got one mother, but you got one heart, and I'm trying to not have a heart attack. I got one mind, and I'm not trying to be in nobody's psychotic war."[6]

Moesha's language conveys that remaining in close contact with her mother posed genuine threats to her physical and mental health. Detachment was not a preference. It was a survival strategy. This framing of detachment as self-protection was present across all seventeen daughters' accounts. They emphasized that creating distance was not about punishing their mothers or expressing anger, though frustration was often present. It was about preventing further harm to themselves. Through detachment, daughters prioritized their own needs and well-being, even when doing so violated cultural expectations of selfless maternal devotion.

The language of protection also appeared in how daughters described what they were protecting themselves from. Lisa explained her need to be mindful about what she allows into her emotional space, indicating that detachment also functions as boundary-setting:

"I don't figure out her situation when she's in an emotional crisis… It makes me think of who I'm putting first and what I'm letting in. Am I letting toxicity in? I need to be more aware of how I feel."[7]

Functional View of Mothers

For several daughters, detachment involved redefining the maternal relationship in purely functional or biological terms. They did not view their mothers as sources of emotional support, guidance, or love. Instead, daughters acknowledged them simply as the women who gave birth to them. This redefinition allowed daughters to release expectations that their mothers could not or would not meet. Joy articulated this clearly:

"I mean, she's my mom. She's alive. But… we don't have that connection."[8]

Joy's statement acknowledges biological reality without suggesting an emotional bond, explaining how the relationship is reduced to a factual status rather than a felt connection. Moesha went further, explicitly rejecting the maternal title, stripping the relationship of any emotional or relational content:

"That is not my mother. She is my egg donor."[9]

Moesha's language conveys that her mother's role in her life does not extend beyond biological function. Jen described a similar redefinition:

"I don't call her 'Mommy,' 'Mama,' or anything like that. She is my mother. Period. She's the person who birthed me and is on my birth certificate."[10]

The distinction Jen draws between affectionate terms like "Mommy" and the formal "mother" reflects emotional distancing enacted through language. For daughters like Jen, Moesha, and Joy, mothers are acknowledged as the person who performed the biological act of giving birth, but they are not claimed as "mom" in any deeper sense. This functional redefinition served as a protective mechanism for daughters. If you no longer expect your mother to provide emotional support, you cannot be disappointed when she fails to do so. If you view her solely as a biological relation rather than a parental figure, her inability or unwillingness to mother you becomes less personally wounding. The redefinition does not erase the pain of what was never received, but it adjusts expectations to align with reality.[11]

Across these varied personal definitions—emotional disconnection, protection and self-preservation, functional redefinition—what unified daughters' understanding was that detachment represented an adaptive, self-protective response to harmful maternal relationships. It was their choice to prioritize their own well-being when their mothers could not or would not do so.

Cultural Meanings: Navigating Black Family Expectations

While daughters' personal definitions of detachment centered on emotional disconnection and self-protection, their understandings of what detachment meant culturally were far more complex and sometimes contradictory. Fifteen of the seventeen daughters acknowledged that their decision to detach could not be understood apart from the cultural messages that shaped how they were raised and how they viewed maternal relationships.[12] These cultural messages emphasized family loyalty, respect for elders, and reverence for mothers. Mya noted:

"I was taught and told, 'This is your family. You don't cut these people off because you need them.'"[13]

Jen also shed light on this cultural nuance:

"People are currently talking about me and how I've made the decision to detach from my mother and the rest of my family. I'm part of the African-American community… It is what it is."[14]

Daughters went on to discuss how they were specifically exposed to messages on respectability that implied they were expected to endure hardship, even at the hands of their mother. Hope mentioned:

"We often hear, 'Well, that's just your mom, or that's just so and so', … It justifies or excuses certain behaviors."[15]

Considering how most Black daughters are culturally indoctrinated, detaching from a mother is not just a personal decision. For the Sagacious Seventeen, it was a culturally loaded act that daughters interpreted in multiple, sometimes conflicting ways.[16]

Agreeing With Cultural Norms But Choosing to Detach Anyway

Some daughters, particularly those who were born and raised in the South, internalized cultural beliefs that detaching from your mother is inherently disrespectful or wrong. Yet they maintained their detachment despite this belief. These daughters lived in tension. They accepted that they were violating cultural expectations while insisting that their well-being required that violation. Jada articulated this clearly:

"Culturally, detaching means disrespect. That's the only word that comes to mind. Culturally, it's just disrespectful to say you don't want to be in an elder's life. And because we're talking about my mom specifically, detaching means disrespect."[17]

Jada does not challenge the cultural interpretation. She agrees that detachment is disrespectful, and she chooses it anyway because the alternative, remaining in close contact with her mother, is intolerable. Her detachment is not an act of resistance against cultural norms. It is an act of self-preservation despite those norms. Corrine expressed similar acceptance of cultural judgment:

"I think that it's probably the worst thing ever culturally."[18]

She recognizes that within Black cultural frameworks, detaching from your mother is one of the most serious violations a daughter can commit. Similar to Jada, Corrine maintains her detachment without regret. The tension she lives with is the knowledge that her community may view her as doing something unconscionable, even as she knows it was necessary for her survival. This group of daughters carried internal conflict and guilt in some cases. They were socialized to believe that good daughters do not abandon their mothers, and "that's still ya mama" is reason enough to endure any harm. They could not fully shake those beliefs, even as they acted against them. Younger Black Southern daughters, particularly those in their twenties and early thirties, were most likely to express guilt. Charity admitted:

"I feel like a really sh*tty person, sometimes, that I feel this way about my mom."[19]

The fact that Charity feels bad not only about her decision to detach, but also about her feelings toward her mother reveals how deeply cultural messages about maternal devotion are internalized. She judges herself for not wanting a close relationship with her mother, even though that relationship has been harmful. Hope discussed the generational and regional factors that intensified this guilt:

"Being of the generation where we are not excusing certain behaviors, it's already hard enough… especially being a person of color with a very Southern family."[20]

Hope recognizes that her generation, Gen Z, is more willing to prioritize boundaries and mental health over family loyalty, but that shift does not erase the cultural conditioning she received growing up in a Southern Black family where respect for elders and maternal devotion were non-negotiable values.

For these daughters, detachment was never a simple decision. It was not chosen lightly, nor without conflict or cost. It required them to live with the weight of cultural disapproval, internal guilt, and the painful awareness that their choices would be misunderstood by those who raised them to believe that loyalty to family must come at any price. Yet they chose themselves anyway. Their stories reveal that detachment is not always the rejection of culture, but sometimes the heartbreaking acknowledgment that your well-being requires what culture forbids. They carry the tension of loving their mothers, honoring their heritage, and protecting their own lives, all at once. And in that tension, they embody a quiet but profound truth: Sometimes the most difficult form of respect is telling the truth about harm.

Detaching as Cultural Resistance

In contrast to daughters who internalized cultural norms and felt guilty for violating them, another group consciously rejected those norms. These daughters viewed detachment as an act of resistance against cultural expectations they believed were harmful. They broke away from expectations that required Black daughters to endure mistreatment in the name of family loyalty. They decided not to prioritize their mothers' needs over their own well-being, nor did these daughters choose to remain silent about maternal harm. Twelve out of seventeen daughters described consciously challenging traditional notions of unquestioned family loyalty, framing detachment as necessary boundary-setting rather than disrespect. Moesha expressed this perspective forcefully:

"Culturally, in the Black community, baby, you only get one mom. Honor your parents for your days will be long on the earth… I honor her by keeping my distance. She [has provoked] me, you gotta say [all the Scripture] together. I don't give a d*mn about the culture."[21]

Moesha acknowledges the cultural and biblical mandates around honoring mothers, but she reinterprets what honor means. For her, honoring her mother involves keeping a distance to prevent herself from being provoked into dishonoring behavior. She explicitly rejects cultural pressure, asserting that her wellbeing takes precedence over cultural conformity. Destiny articulated a similar rejection of cultural norms around unconditional respect for elders:

"You have to give [respect] to get it. Whether you are older than me or an elder. If you're going to disrespect me… I'm going to get disrespectful. And I don't believe in, 'Oh, that's your elder, that's your auntie,' I don't give a d*mn who you are. Was I your daughter? Was I your sister? Was I your cousin when you did whatever you did to me?"[22]

Destiny's words challenge the one-directional respect model that characterizes many Black family dynamics, where children and younger generations are expected to show deference regardless of how elders treat them. Daughters like Destiny insist on reciprocity. They demanded mutual respect because, to them, being an elder or a mother does not entitle someone to abuse or disrespect without consequences.

For this group of daughters, breaking expectations of loyalty and respectability was not a sign of disrespect but a commitment to breaking intergenerational cycles of harm that had been normalized within families. They refused to accept cultural messages that expected them to tolerate abuse, neglect, or chronic mistreatment. They viewed cultural norms that demanded unconditional maternal loyalty as complicit in enabling harmful mothering.[23] These daughters often expressed frustration with how cultural loyalty is weaponized against Black daughters who attempt to set boundaries. Jasmine explained:

"When I think about the older generation, detaching is disrespectful. You don't do it. You only get one family, and that's the same rhetoric that my mom uses."[24]

She recognizes that her mother deploys cultural expectations as a tool to prevent accountability. By insisting "you only get one family," her mother attempts to foreclose any possibility that Jasmine might choose to create distance.

Daughters who detached as an act of resistance embodied something particular. They had the clarity of knowing they were making a choice, acknowledging the weight and implications of making it anyway, and stood ten toes down on their decision. These daughters were adamant about not allowing cultural loyalty to function as a reason to remain in harm's way. This was their stance, after counting the cost. These daughters lost relationships, have been the subject of family narratives, and are labeled as "the difficult one", "the ungrateful one", or "the daughter who abandoned her mother". However, what these daughters convey is that you have permission choose yourself, and in doing so, you're not betraying your culture. Instead, you have the opportunity to transform it.

Detaching as a Cultural Norm

A smaller but notable group of daughters offered a third interpretation. They do not see maternal detachment as a deviation from Black culture, but as a cultural pattern, an inherited response to intergenerational trauma. These daughters argued that emotional distance between Black mothers and daughters is common, despite how it traditionally has not been discussed openly. Amina articulated this perspective most clearly:

"Being detached from your parents is Black culture. It is a rite of passage."[25]

From Amina's view, the pattern of maternal emotional unavailability and daughters' subsequent detachment has been transmitted across generations of Black families, rooted in historical trauma.

She elaborated:

"I think it's deeply ingrained generational trauma for all of us. I could think all the way back to slavery and having your kids ripped away from you with no choice. I can see how, over time, that looks like not getting emotionally invested, doing the bare minimum, or doing what they say you are supposed to do so that you do not get arrested, or don't raise any alarms or cause any room for extra attention."[26]

Amina traces maternal emotional distance back to slavery, when Black mothers could not afford to become deeply attached to children who might be sold away from them at any moment. That historical trauma likely created protective detachment, a strategy for survival that involved withholding emotion to guard against inevitable loss. According to Amina, this pattern was passed down through generations, evolving from a response to specific historical conditions into a general relational template. Brooklyn supported this interpretation from her own observations:

"In my friend group alone, nobody has a relationship with their mother that I envy. Even females that I know, no one has said, 'I love my mom so much.' Everybody's just like, 'My mom was just there, and that's it.'"[27]

Brooklyn's account suggests that emotionally distant maternal relationships are far more common than often acknowledged. They are, in her and Amina's experience, the norm. Mothers who are "just there", physically present but emotionally unavailable, are common enough that Brooklyn does not know anyone with a close, warm maternal relationship to envy.

The perspective of detaching being a cultural norm does not excuse maternal harm or suggest that emotional distance is inevitable. It provides a framework for understanding why so many Black mothers struggle with emotional presence. If detachment is a culturally transmitted response to trauma, then individual mothers are not solely responsible for patterns they inherited and did not choose. This does not eliminate accountability. It contextualizes their limitations. The daughters who held this view tended to express more empathy toward their mothers, recognizing them as products of systems and histories that constrained their capacity for emotional connection. They still chose detachment for their own well-being, but they framed it less as resistance and more as continuation of an inherited pattern they were trying, through their own healing work, to interrupt.

Practical Detachment Strategies

Understanding what detachment means, personally and culturally, provides necessary context, but meaning alone does not capture how daughters actually enacted it in their daily lives. Detachment was not merely an internal shift in perspective or feeling. It was a set of lived practices that required continuous negotiation, emotional labor, and sustained effort. For the Sagacious Seventeen, detachment was not a single decision made once and then completed. It was an ongoing process. They had to determine what level of contact they could tolerate, what boundaries were necessary for their well-being, and how to maintain those boundaries within family systems that often resisted or refused to respect their need for distance. Detachment required vigilance. It required renegotiating roles, expectations, and patterns of interaction that had been established over a lifetime. Among the daughters, three maintained a complete cutoff from their mothers. They had no contact whatsoever, no expectation of a future relationship, and a firm commitment to maintaining permanent separation. The remaining fourteen maintained some form of limited contact, though they emphasized that this contact was highly controlled, emotionally bound, and sustained more out of obligation, cultural expectation, or practical necessity than genuine relational desire.[28]

Complete Cutoff

For the three daughters who chose complete severance, this decision represented the culmination of a long process of recognition. They came to understand that any contact with their mothers was harmful and that a relationship with them could not exist without threatening their emotional or physical well-being. Complete cutoff was not described as impulsive rejection or punishment. Rather, it was framed as a necessary intervention to preserve their mental health, restore a sense of safety, and interrupt cycles of harm that had persisted for years. These daughters described reaching a point where continued engagement was no longer sustainable, and where the costs of contact consistently outweighed any potential benefit. Their decision reflects the most definitive form of detachment described in this study, one grounded not in rejection of motherhood itself, but in the recognition that proximity to their mothers required the ongoing sacrifice of their well-being. Moesha explained:

"I buried my mother. So, you know, so if somebody called me right now and said that she died, I'll say okay. I don't dig up graves."[29]

Moesha's language of burial conveys the finality of her decision. The relationship is dead, mourned, and finished. She has no intention of revisiting it under any circumstances. Joy explained her complete cutoff in terms of the absence of a bond:

"I have no desire to keep her in the loop with my life. I detach because there is no bond there."[30]

Without an emotional connection, there was no relationship to maintain. Joy did not experience her cutoff as a loss because what she severed was something that had never truly existed in the first place. Diana's complete cutoff was tied to physical separation from the cult her mother remained part of:

"I left her with [the cult leader], and I went completely no contact. It was horrible."[31]

For Diana, maintaining any contact with her mother would have required engaging with an abusive system she had escaped. A complete cutoff was necessary for her physical, psychological, and spiritual safety. These daughters did not waver in their decisions. They did not check in periodically to see if their mothers had changed. They did not leave room for reconciliation. They had closed the door and were at peace with keeping it that way.

Limited Contact

The fourteen daughters who maintained limited contact described a range of deliberate strategies for managing their relationships in ways that protected their well-being while allowing for some degree of continued engagement. Unlike a complete cutoff, limited contact required constant negotiation. It demanded emotional discipline, intentional boundary-setting, and ongoing monitoring of what felt safe. These daughters did not experience continued contact as effortless or natural. Rather, it was carefully structured through a range of practices.

Emotional distancing, the practice of withholding vulnerability even when in physical proximity to others, was one of the most prevalent detachment practices for these daughters. They learned to present a controlled version of themselves, one that could not be easily criticized, dismissed, or wounded. This distance created a protective barrier, allowing them to remain present without fully exposing themselves to relational harm. Corrine mentioned:

"I don't share my joy with my mother."[32]

She might see her mother at family gatherings or participate in surface-level conversation, but she keeps her mother at arm's length emotionally. Her mother does not get access to what brings Corrine happiness. Their relationship exists functionally — they are civil, they fulfill family obligations — but there is no intimacy.

Several daughters emphasized that they no longer seek support from their mothers. Hope expressed:

"I know a lot of people who will call their mothers if something happens. But for me? I'm going to fight tooth and nail. I will figure it out. I will cry, die, crawl, whatever I need to do. I'm not picking up the phone to call my mother first."[33]

Daughters, like Hope, completely reorient who they turn to in a crisis. This redirection of support-seeking is a critical component of emotional detachment, recognizing that the person who should be your primary source of comfort cannot fulfill that role and finding others who can.

Physical boundaries also played a role in how daughters managed limited contact. Some chose to live in different geographic locations from their mothers, creating physical distance that made frequent interaction impossible. Others limited the duration of phone calls or visits, ensuring that exposure to their mothers was time-limited. Some avoided one-on-one interactions, engaging with their mothers only in group settings where other family members provided buffers. Shandra described how she and her sister rotate caregiving responsibilities for their mother while protecting themselves through structured separation:

"My sister and I take turns in the caregiving. There are some weeks I'm like, 'Hey, I'm blocking mom on my cell phone. You know, this is your week', and vice versa. So, we're here to be a buffer for each other from her and say your mama is a mess."[34]

All of the daughters who have limited contact with their mothers described this kind of boundary; carefully monitoring when, how, and for how long to interact with their mothers was essential. Jada explained her approach:

"If it comes to the point where I feel disrespected, or it's not going anywhere, I'm very honest and quick to say this isn't working for me. I don't want to talk to you anymore, and the conversation is over for me, and I don't feel any remorse about it."[35]

Daughters, like Jada, do not endure interactions that become harmful. The moment a boundary is crossed, they exit without guilt. This requires both clarity about limits and confidence in enforcing them. Daughters described learning to recognize early warning signs of conflict and withdrawing before situations escalated; they discerned when conversations were heading toward dangerous territory, or when interactions had reached the limit of what they could tolerate. This hyperawareness, while exhausting, allowed daughters to protect themselves proactively.[36]

The Complexity of Detachment

What emerges from this study is that detachment cannot be reduced to a single definition or interpretation. It is not simply distance, nor merely rejection. It is both a continuation of inherited patterns of emotional separation and an interruption of those patterns through conscious boundary-setting. For some daughters, detachment was framed as disrespect, a violation of cultural expectations surrounding loyalty, honor, and motherhood. For several, it felt like resistance — a refusal to continue cycles of harm that stretched across generations. Still, there were a few who experienced it not as a choice at all, but as reality, an unavoidable response to relationships that could no longer sustain them.

The layered meanings of detachment reveal the complexity of strained Black mother–daughter relationships. These were not simple conflicts with clear beginnings or easy resolutions. For the Sagacious Seventeen, detachment became a way of living with what could not be repaired, at least for the time being. It was a strategy for protecting what remained of their well-being. Ultimately, detachment was not the absence of relationship but its redefinition. It was the boundary drawn where hope met reality. It was the moment daughters chose themselves when their mothers could not, or would not, choose them.

6

Relief & Rupture

The Paradox of Detachment

Choosing to detach from your mother does not arrive with a clean feeling. You expect relief and find grief waiting alongside it. You anticipate gaining clarity and then experience sorrow. The daughters in this study lived in a paradox: Detachment was a necessary act that came with an undeniable cost. Creating distance protected them from ongoing harm, but it could not undo the harm already inflicted. Detachment brought safety, yet it also exposed loss. It brought a sense of ease, yet it demanded mourning. In this way, detachment functioned as both a solution and a revelation. It addressed the immediate problem of continued injury while making visible the accumulated pain of the past.

This chapter turns to RQ3, which asks: How did Black adult women describe how detaching from their Black mothers impacts them? The study's findings related to this question boil down to this: Two seemingly opposing realities can exist at the same time. It was an act of self-preservation that also required daughters to confront the reality of the mothering they did not receive. For many of them, they were no longer struggling for maternal connection in the same way, but they were now grieving the relationship they had hoped for and

the mother they needed but did not have. [1] This
grief was not tied to physical death but to relational
loss, a form of mourning complicated by the fact
that their mother was still alive. Therefore,
detachment required the Sagacious Seventeen to
hold both peace and pain in the same hands.

Emotional Freedom and Liberation

The most immediate and pronounced emotion
many daughters described was freedom. They felt
released from the constant emotional weight of
their mothers' expectations, criticisms, moods, and
demands. Destiny articulated this sense of
liberation:

"I feel free. It's a liberating feeling. I don't have
anything standing in my way or holding me back. I
get to be myself and be free and show up for
myself the way I need to be shown up for…"[2]

Destiny's words capture what freedom meant for
many daughters. It gave them the ability to finally
prioritize themselves without guilt, exist without
someone constantly undermining their sense of
worth, and make choices based on their own needs
rather than their mothers' demands. Freedom was
not just the absence of constraint. It was the
presence of possibility. The ability to explore who
they were when not defined by maternal approval
or disapproval. Corrine described her experience of
freedom in terms of released pressure:

"[I feel] freedom and less pressure. I can stop
wondering and stop trying to meet this awesome
daughter. I can just… let it go."[3]

For Corrine, detachment meant she could finally stop performing the role of perfect daughter, stop striving to be enough for someone who would never be satisfied. The relief of releasing that impossible standard was palpable in her words. This newfound freedom manifested as release from being engulfed in their mothers' emotions and crises. Many daughters shared how, before detachment, they had functioned as emotional support systems for their mothers.[4] This consisted of absorbing their mothers' pain, managing their mothers' feelings, and prioritizing their mothers' needs above their own. Detachment ended that dynamic. Several daughters also discussed the freedom of no longer anticipating conflict or walking on eggshells. When you are closely connected to someone who is emotionally volatile, you constantly monitor moods, adjust your behavior to avoid triggering one's anger, and brace yourself for the next explosion; it is exhausting work. Detachment allowed daughters to finally relax and exist without the anxiety that had characterized their relationships with their mothers.

Peace and Clarity

Alongside freedom came peace, a quality many daughters had not experienced while maintaining close contact with their mothers. They described feeling calmer and less consumed by maternal drama. The mental space previously occupied by managing their mothers' emotions or processing maternal criticism was now available for other things, such as their own goals, relationships, and personal healing. The peace was not just emotional but cognitive. Daughters reported being able to think more clearly once they created distance.[5] The fog of constant emotional reactivity lifted. They could see their relationships and themselves more objectively. They understood how much energy they had been expending trying to earn maternal love that was never forthcoming. They saw how deeply the relationships had shaped their sense of self, often in harmful ways. Charity articulated the self-awareness that accompanied detachment:

"I had to sit back and think, who are you outside of your mom? I am so much more self-aware, almost to a fault."[6]

The question "Who are you outside of your mom?" is significant. For daughters who had spent their entire lives shaped by maternal expectations and criticism, detachment created the first real opportunity to explore identity independent of those forces. Charity's self-awareness, while sometimes uncomfortable, represented a form of clarity that had been impossible while enmeshed with her mother. Mya expressed a similar sentiment about reclaiming time and space for herself:

"I have a lot more time for myself. I have a lot more time to live my life and actually do the things that I love and not have to hear [my mother's] voice!"[7]

The relief in Mya's statement is evident. Detachment permitted her to pursue joy without maternal interference or judgment. For many daughters, the clarity extended to understanding their own desires.[8] When you grow up trying to please a mother who cannot be pleased, you often lose track of what you actually want. Your energy goes into anticipating what will earn approval or avoid criticism, not into exploring your own preferences and aspirations. Detachment created space for daughters to ask themselves what they wanted. Not what their mothers wanted for them, not what would make their mothers proud, but what they themselves valued and desired.

Physical Relief

The relief daughters experienced was not only psychological, but it was also physical. Several of them referenced the embodied sensations of lightness, release of tension, and ease in their bodies after detaching from their mothers. This aligns with research on trauma and the body, which demonstrates that chronic stress and relational harm get stored somatically, manifesting as physical tension, pain, and illness.[9] Moesha articulated this physical dimension powerfully:

"I used to have a heaviness on my chest. Just a heaviness. It felt like just pressure. I just feel lightness now. Even on my darkest day, I still feel lighter than what it was."[10]

The image of heaviness on the chest—a physical weight pressing down—captures how the stress of the maternal relationship was not just emotionally but physically oppressive. Moesha's description of feeling lighter "even on my darkest day" reveals that the relief was profound and persistent. Even when she struggled emotionally, the physical burden of the relationship was no longer crushing her.

Other daughters described sleeping better, experiencing less anxiety-related physical symptoms, or simply feeling more at ease in their bodies. Detachment allowed their nervous systems to regulate and their bodies to relax.[11] This physical relief was particularly striking because it revealed how deeply the maternal relationships had affected daughters at every level. The weight they carried was literal, not just metaphorical. And detachment, while not solving all their problems, removed a significant source of chronic stress.

No Regret, And Still Mourning the Mother Wound That Remains

The Sagacious Seventeen made it clear that there were no regrets about detaching from their mothers because the decision was necessary. The absence of regret did not mean the absence of pain, though. Daughters could know with certainty that detachment was right and still mourn what it represented. They could be at peace with their decision while carrying sadness about the circumstances that made the decision necessary. Overall, daughters did not question whether detachment was justified, and many grieved that it had been necessary in the first place.[12]

The Persistence of Grief

Daughters described a range of emotions that surfaced after choosing to detach: sadness, anger, grief, and longing.[13] These emotions were not fleeting reactions to the decision to detach. They were ongoing, persistent reminders that their mother wound had not been resolved simply by creating physical or emotional distance. Many daughters grieved the mothers they lost, and the mothers they had never had. Hope articulated this poignantly:

"I heard a Black woman on TikTok say, 'I hate that I don't want my mother, but I need my mother,' and I feel that. There's a lot of growth in womanhood I get sad about."[14]

Hope's statement captures the paradox many daughters live: Not wanting a relationship with their actual mothers (because those relationships were harmful) and desperately needing mothering (since the human need for maternal love and guidance does not disappear just because your mother cannot or will not provide it).

Diana described missing a version of her mother that existed only in early childhood:

"I miss the mom I had before I was 10 years old. I used to go and sit on my mom's lap and, you know, go and lie with her and all kinds of stuff. Like she was actually kind of cool."[15]

Diana's grief was for a mother who had once been present, affectionate, and safe. A mother who disappeared and was replaced by someone, whom

Diana eventually had to leave for her own survival. The loss was compounded. She lost the loving mother of her early childhood, and she lost the possibility that the mother she had back then would ever return.

This grief that Hope and Diana described can be a surprising feeling for daughters after they choose to detach. For the daughters who expect relief and, instead, find themselves crying, it is a sign that they needed their mothers back then and now. Grief after detachment is a good sign. Why? It means they stopped pretending the loss was not real.

Watching Mothers Show Up for Others

One of the most aching experiences daughters described was watching their mothers demonstrate care and affection for other people while not extending it towards them.[16] This took multiple forms: mothers being attentive to siblings, mothers showing up for friends or extended family, and most painfully, mothers being loving grandmothers to daughters' children.

Jasmine expressed the envy and confusion this created:

"There's a part of me, recently, that has started to feel a little bit of envy or jealousy. I'm not sure which one, but that she can show up for my grandmother..."[17]

Watching her mother care for her aging grandmother in ways she had never cared for Jasmine raised the question: "If you are capable of showing up, why didn't you show up for me?"

Amina articulated similar pain:

"I'm angry. I've seen her change for other people. I get to watch her love the people around her in the way that I want to be loved."[18]

The anger Amina describes is rooted in witnessing evidence that her mother possesses the capacity for love and care. She is not fundamentally incapable, but she chose not to offer that to her daughter. This suggests to Amina that she was not worthy of her mother's best self, that she somehow did not merit the treatment her mother readily gives others.

For daughters who are mothers themselves, watching their own mothers be affectionate, patient, and engaged grandmothers was particularly wrenching. Shandra described this experience:

"I saw how gentle, how protective she was with my daughter… at first it was hurtful because I was like, oh, you didn't have the capacity [for me when I was a child]."[19]

Shandra's use of "at first" suggests she eventually came to terms with this reality, but the initial hurt of seeing her mother treat her daughter with tenderness she had never received cut deeply. It confirmed that her mother had always possessed the capacity for gentle mothering. She simply had not chosen to mother Shandra that way.

Corrine expressed an even more acute pain:

"And watching her grandmother, my child…, [my mom] seems so natural and good at it. So, why did you not mother me? You have the ability to do this. Why did you choose not to? The more children that I've had over time, she just keeps being this awesome grandmother, and then she just keeps being a worse and worse mother to me."[20]

The contrast Corrine describes — awesome grandmother, terrible mother — creates cognitive and emotional dissonance. If her mother can be patient, loving, and engaged with her grandchildren, why couldn't she be that way with Corrine? The answer, painful as it is, seems to be that she chose not to.

Envy and Comparison

Beyond watching their own mothers show up for others, many daughters described a painful envy when witnessing other women with close, loving maternal relationships. Diana stated:

"I have resentment and jealousy of women who have a close relationship with their mother. Guys too. My husband has an excellent relationship with his mom."[21]

Being in proximity to people who have what you desperately want but cannot have is its own form of grief. Every Mother's Day post on social media, every conversation where friends casually mention calling their moms for advice, and every wedding where a bride gets ready with her mother become reminders of absence.

Some daughters articulated that they wished they had a different kind of mother. Brooklyn explained:

"My mother wasn't horrible. She just isn't the mother I want."[22]

Her statement reflects a particular kind of longing. The quiet longing of never having a mother who truly saw her or made her feel cherished. Her mother was present and functional, not actively harmful. She was not the mother Brooklyn needed, though. Other daughters were more direct, expressing that they wished they had a different mother entirely because of the severity of harm they experienced.

Then there were daughters like Jasmine, who clarified:

"I don't wish I had a different mom. I just wish my mom were more maternal."[23]

Jasmine's distinction is important. She does not want to erase her mother and replace her with someone else. She wants her mother to be different, to possess the capacity to nurture, be tender, and present.

These expressions of envy, comparison, and longing reveal that detachment did not eliminate desire for mothering. It simply made clear that their desire would not be fulfilled by the women who birthed them. Daughters had to find ways to mother themselves. Some sought motherly advice and nurturance from other women—grandmothers, fictive kin, mentors, older sorors, therapists, church mothers—while others decided to live with the unfilled longing.

Younger Daughters: The Inner Child's Yearning

The longing for mothering was particularly pronounced among younger daughters in their twenties and early thirties.[24] These women were more likely to acknowledge openly that their inner child — the part of them that was still the little girl who needed her mother — yearned for maternal connection even as their adult selves knew that connection was impossible or unsafe.

Hope shared her experience of this yearning in the context of witnessing friends receive maternal support during major life transitions:

"My friend had a baby. Her mom and her mother-in-law were by her side. And I was like, oh, it's beautiful. But days afterward, I was in a lot of pain. It's beautiful to see, but I don't have that relationship with my mother."[25]

Hope's pain was visceral, triggered by witnessing what she did not have. Seeing her friend supported by both her mother and mother-in-law during childbirth made visible the absence in Hope's own life. She could appreciate the beauty of that support for her friend while grieving that she would never receive it from her own mother.

Charity expressed similar anticipatory grief about future milestones:

"I really wish I could have a better relationship with my mom, especially now, but like even in the future, for whenever I have children, because grandparents are awesome, and I would hate for my kids to not have them."[26]

Charity's wish is not just for herself, but also for her future children. She mourns in advance the grandmother they will not have, or will have only in a limited, supervised capacity.

The younger daughters' yearning often coexisted with greater openness to reconciliation, should circumstances change. They had not fully closed the door. They maintained some hope, however faint, that their mothers might do the work necessary to make relationships possible. Amina shared:

"I want a better relationship with my mom. But I'm also accepting of the fact that it may not happen before she leaves this earth."[27]

For daughters like Amina, this hope made their grief more acute because it meant they lived in the tension of wanting something they probably would never have.

Older Daughters: Acceptance and Finality

In contrast, older daughters, particularly those in their late thirties and forties, tended to express more acceptance and less active yearning.[28] They had lived longer with the reality of who their mothers were. They had spent more years trying, hoping, and being disappointed. This group of daughters had fully grieved the mothers they would never have and had made peace with that loss. This does not mean older daughters felt no pain. Rather, the quality of their pain was different, less raw longing, and more settled sorrow. These daughters accepted that their mothers would not change, making reconciliation unlikely, which indicated they would likely navigate the rest of their lives without maternal support. That acceptance brought its own form of peace, even as it acknowledged permanent loss. Several older daughters described a shift from hoping their mothers would become different to simply accepting them as they were.[29] This acceptance did not mean approving of their mothers' behavior or excusing harm. It meant releasing the expectation that mothers would ever be capable of showing up differently.

The generational difference in how daughters experienced the mother wound suggests that time, while not healing the wound entirely, does shift how it is carried. Younger daughters were still in active grief, wrestling with desire, and hoping against hope that something might change. Older daughters had moved into a different stage. They were not beyond sorrow but into a grief that had been integrated into their lives rather than overwhelming them.

The Unresolved Nature of the Wound

What becomes clear across daughters' reflections is that detachment does not resolve the pain of being unmothered. Creating distance provides relief from ongoing harm, but it cannot undo what has already been done. Detachment cannot fill the void left by absent or inadequate mothering, and it cannot restore what was never given. Thus, the wounds of the past and present become more apparent and require intentional healing.

Ironically, detachment is a condition that makes healing possible. By removing the ongoing source of harm, detachment creates an opportunity for daughters to address the wounds that had long been overshadowed by the constant labor of managing their maternal relationships. However, tending to those wounds necessitates something difficult. It requires daughters to feel them fully. They must acknowledge the depth of what was lost, and, in many cases, what was never present at all. This is why detachment, while necessary and beneficial, is also painful. It strips away the defenses daughters once relied upon to survive their childhoods: minimization ("it wasn't that bad"), rationalization ("she did her best"), and hope ("maybe she'll change"). Without these protective layers, daughters are left to confront a reality that is often unbearable in its clarity. The reality is that they were not adequately loved, protected, or nurtured by the women who should have loved them most. That recognition is devastating. And detachment, by creating distance, makes it impossible to turn away from it.

III

The Work of Becoming

7

Healing in Motion

The Healing Work Daughters Are Doing

Healing is what came after the Sagacious Seventeen decided to detach. Healing requires the slow, nonlinear work of becoming someone less defined by what was done to you. The daughters in this study chose that work. They did not do it perfectly. They did not do it quickly, but they did it with intention, and this is what this chapter is about. Detachment did not mark the end of the daughters' journeys. It was the onset of a new beginning. This chapter continues the exploration of RQ3 by examining how daughters responded to the emotional and psychological impact of detachment. It presents what emerged from their narratives: Black women who refused to accept that the wounds inflicted in childhood had to define the trajectory of their lives. They were choosing differently: prioritizing awareness over silence, growth over repetition, and restoration over resignation.

During their interviews, the Sagacious Seventeen reflected on their active healing journeys. They described the practices they engaged in, the self-awareness they cultivated, the behavioral changes they pursued, the communities that sustained them, and the commitment to generational restoration that motivated their

108

efforts.[1] In choosing to heal, these daughters began interrupting cycles that had persisted across generations. Their healing work took many forms but was unified in purpose. Daughters sought to transform the impact of maternal harm, develop healthier ways of relating to themselves and others, and ensure that patterns of emotional neglect, criticism, and unavailability would not continue through them. The following are not accounts of complete resolution, but of healing in motion: women learning, unlearning, rebuilding, and reclaiming themselves in the aftermath of maternal disconnection.

Therapy as Foundation

For most daughters, therapy was not optional; it was essential. Fourteen out of the seventeen were in therapy at the time of the interviews, with several attending weekly sessions where they processed their maternal relationships, worked through childhood trauma, and developed skills for emotional regulation and healthy forms of coping.[2] Therapy provided a space where they could speak truths they had been taught to suppress, express anger they had been told was inappropriate, and grieve losses they had been expected to get over. Michelle described the role therapy played in her healing:

"I've actually been in therapy weekly since that incident with my mother."[3]

The incident Michelle referenced was one of many, but it was the catalyst that made her recognize she needed professional support to process the accumulated harm. Therapy gave daughters tools they had never been taught. They learned to identify and challenge cognitive distortions—the faulty thinking patterns that had been shaped by maternal criticism and neglect.[4] They learned that their feelings were valid, and their needs mattered. They learned to set boundaries, recognize unhealthy relational patterns, and distinguish between what belonged to them and what belonged to their mothers. For daughters who had internalized beliefs about their inadequacy, therapy became a space to dismantle those beliefs. When you have been told repeatedly that you are not good enough or that your emotions are too much, those messages become embedded in your psyche. Therapy provided counter-narratives. Therapists reflected daughters' worth, validated their pain, and helped them see that the problem was not them, but what had been done to them. Additionally, many daughters emphasized that finding the right therapist, particularly a Black therapist who understood the cultural context of their experiences, was crucial. They needed therapists who would not minimize the harm of maternal relationships, push premature forgiveness or reconciliation, and understand the specific pressures Black daughters face around family loyalty and respectability. When daughters found therapists who could hold all of that complexity, therapy became transformative.

Beyond the Therapy Room

While therapy was central, daughters also engaged in other healing practices that supported their journeys. Several described using journaling as a way to process emotions, track patterns, and give voice to feelings they could not yet speak aloud.[5] Writing created distance. They could see their experiences on the page rather than only feeling them internally. This externalization helped them gain clarity about what they had endured and what they needed to heal. Reading was another significant practice. Charity mentioned:

"I started reading all these books to try to make myself better… What Happened to You by Bruce Perry helps me think about what my mom went through to act the way she does."[6]

Books on trauma, attachment, childhood emotional neglect, and healing provided frameworks for understanding. They helped daughters recognize that their experiences were not unique because others had walked similar paths, and yet, healing was possible. The knowledge gained from reading validated their pain and offered roadmaps for moving forward. Faith-based practices also played a role for some daughters.[7] Prayer, meditation, reading the Bible, and connection with faith communities provided spiritual grounding and comfort. For daughters who believed in God, the Father of Jesus Christ, their faith offered assurance. It affirmed that they were loved unconditionally and they were valued by the Most High, even when their mothers had failed to do so. These spiritual practices complemented therapeutic work, addressing dimensions of healing that psychology alone could not reach. Some daughters combined multiple healing practices. They built what one might call healing ecosystems, interconnected practices that addressed different aspects of their wounds and supported different facets of their growth. This multifaceted approach reflected the reality that the mother wound was complex and multidimensional, requiring varied interventions to heal.

Confronting Pain

All of these practices required daughters to do something difficult. They had to confront pain rather than avoid it. For years, some had coped by minimizing, compartmentalizing, or staying busy enough that they did not have to feel the depth of their hurt. Healing meant stopping, turning toward the pain, and allowing themselves to fully feel what they had been avoiding. This confrontation was not passive. It was active emotional labor. Daughters had to sit with grief, anger, sadness, and longing. They wrestled with emotions that were overwhelming and often felt endless. They had to revisit childhood memories that some had tried to forget and acknowledge the full extent of what they had lost or never received. This work was exhausting, but the daughters described this confrontation as necessary. You cannot heal what you do not acknowledge, and you cannot process what you refuse to feel. The pain they had carried, and in some ways, still do, for years — sometimes decades — needed to be brought into the light, examined, felt, and gradually released. Avoiding it only prolonged suffering. Facing it created the possibility of transformation.

It is imperative to acknowledge that daughters did not feel everything at once. Healing does not require you to excavate every wound in a single season. But there must be a willingness to begin. You also have to stop moving fast enough that the pain cannot catch you. These daughters teach us to trust that feeling pain, even in small doses, will not destroy us. Many of us have already overcome what wounded us, so you can survive the feeling of it, too.

Developing Self-Awareness: Recognizing Patterns

As daughters engaged in healing work, they developed greater self-awareness.[8] They began to recognize how their maternal relationships shaped their emotional patterns, relational tendencies, and core beliefs about themselves. This recognition was often uncomfortable because it meant seeing clearly how deeply they had been affected by their mothers, but it was also empowering because awareness is the first step toward change.

Emotional Guardedness and Trust Issues

Many daughters recognized that they struggled with trust and emotional vulnerability. Amina articulated this clearly:

"I don't easily form relationships well. Only two women really know me. Everybody else? Absolutely not. I don't trust easily. I also got really used to not needing people."[9]

Amina's emotional guardedness was an adaptation to having a mother she could not trust. If the person who should be most trustworthy proves unreliable, dangerous, or hurtful, you learn to protect yourself by not letting anyone close. For daughters like Amina, this pattern "served" them well in childhood. Emotional guardedness kept them safe from further maternal harm. In adulthood, though, it limited their capacity for intimacy and connection. They kept friends at arm's length, struggled to be vulnerable with romantic partners, and avoided asking for help even when they desperately needed it. The protective mechanism that once was necessary became a barrier to the very connection they longed for. Recognizing this pattern allowed daughters to begin examining it. They had to determine if emotional guardedness was still serving them or was now limiting them.

Addressing Avoidant Tendencies

Several daughters admitted that they had developed the "cutoff spirit", a tendency to exit relationships or situations at the first sign of conflict or discomfort rather than staying and working through difficulties.[10] This avoidance made sense given their histories. When your mother is volatile, unpredictable, or cruel, you learn to protect yourself by withdrawing before things escalate. In adult relationships where conflict is normal and resolvable, the cutoff spirit became problematic. Daughters would end friendships over minor disagreements, quit jobs when challenges arose, or avoid difficult conversations that needed to happen. They were applying survival strategies from childhood to situations that did not require such extreme responses.

Hope described her journey of recognizing this:

"I was running away from things, and after doing a lot of uncovering myself, trying to learn why I was acting certain ways. And I realized I was running away from my mother."[11]

Hope's insight that she was not only running from her mother, but from anything that was a reminder of her maternal dynamics, allowed her to distinguish between situations that genuinely required distance from those where staying and engaging would serve her better. Daughters talked about other avoidant tendencies, such as staying excessively busy to avoid feeling, overachieving to prove worth, or focusing on others' problems to avoid confronting their own pain. These patterns kept daughters functional yet prevented them from accessing the vulnerability and stillness necessary for deep healing. Recognizing them was the first step toward choosing differently.

Perfectionism and People-Pleasing

Daughters acknowledged that they struggled with perfectionism — the belief that they had to be flawless to be acceptable — and people-pleasing — the compulsion to prioritize others' needs and comfort over their own. Both patterns stemmed from childhoods in which maternal love and approval felt conditional on performance. If you grow up believing that your mother will only love you if you are perfect, there is a chance that you internalize the belief that your worth is tied to achievement, compliance, or meeting others' expectations. You can become hypervigilant about others' reactions, constantly adjusting your behavior to earn approval. You may even struggle to say, "no", so you do not disappoint people, even if it means you de-prioritize your own needs. Overall, with perfectionism and people-pleasing, you risk exhausting yourself by trying to be enough.

Daughters who recognized these patterns began to ask themselves hard questions:

"Whose approval am I seeking?"

"Am I making choices based on what I want or what others expect?"

"What would it mean to disappoint someone and still know I am worthy?"

"Can I be imperfect and still be loved?"

These were not abstract philosophical questions for these daughters. They were the kinds of questions that arose in ordinary moments — when a friend asked for a favor they did not have the capacity to give, when they were given praise they could not receive gracefully, when they accomplished something significant and waited, almost automatically, for someone to find what was wrong with it. The work of dismantling perfectionism and people-pleasing happened in those ordinary moments, one small choice at a time.

Combatting Negative Self-Talk

Another pattern daughters made note of was harsh internal dialogue, the critical voice in their heads that sounded suspiciously like their mothers.[12] This internalized maternal criticism told them they were not good enough. It was relentless and often unconscious, operating as background noise that undermined their confidence and peace. Becoming aware of this internal critic was revelatory for many daughters. They realized they were now doing to themselves what their mothers had done to them: criticizing, belittling, and holding themselves to impossible standards. Daughters learned to replace the criticism with self-compassion, and this shift was central to healing. Daughters learned, or were still learning, to speak to themselves in the way they would to a beloved friend or their own children, with kindness, patience, and encouragement. They practiced noticing when the critical voice arose and consciously chose a different response, with the hope that the internal dialogue would change. This was slow work. The critical voice did not go away easily or quickly because it had been rehearsed for years. But daughters described moments when they caught it mid-sentence and chose something different. They learned to make a mistake and not spiral. They became courageous enough to look at themselves honestly and, for the first time, without contempt. Those moments accumulated, forming living proof that they did not have to remain at war with themselves.

Learning to Ask for Help

Another critical behavioral change was learning to ask for help.[13] Daughters had been raised, whether by their mothers or the conditions they were in, to be hyper-independent. They learned early on that depending on others was dangerous or futile. Therefore, practicing vulnerable acts of asking for support and allowing others to show up for them made many of them uncomfortable. Asking for help meant admitting they could not do everything alone, and they had to learn to trust that someone would respond with care rather than criticism. But it also meant experiencing the relief of being supported. It allowed them to believe that they did not have to carry everything by themselves, discovering that interdependence is not weakness but wisdom. For daughters who had been raised to need no one, this was quietly revolutionary. To ask for help and have someone show up was, for some of these women, the first time they had proof that their needs were not a burden. That proof did not arrive once and settle the matter. It had to be experienced again and again before it began to feel true.

Showing Up Peacefully

Daughters also described learning to show up more peacefully in their relationships.[14] They were becoming less reactive, less defensive, and less controlled by the emotional patterns formed in their maternal relationships. This is harder than it sounds for women whose nervous systems were trained in homes where conflict was unpredictable, where a mood shift could change the entire atmosphere of a room, and where the safest response to tension was often to either brace, fight back, or flee. Showing up peacefully meant learning to respond from a different place than the one their childhoods had wired them toward. It meant pausing before responding when triggered, noticing the urge to escalate or disappear, and choosing something else. It meant bringing intention to how they interacted with others rather than simply reacting to whatever had been activated. They were learning to feel emotions fully without being controlled by them. Daughters practiced expressing needs clearly without hostility or manipulation and engaged in conflict constructively rather than destructively. They were learning that disagreement did not have to mean danger, that someone being upset did not automatically mean they were under attack, and that they could stay present in discomfort without it becoming catastrophic. These skills take practice and often require ongoing therapeutic support, but they transformed how daughters experienced relationships and how those relationships experienced them.

Embodying What They Longed For

Across these behavioral changes, a theme emerged: Daughters were learning to be for themselves that they had wished their mothers would be for them. They were learning to offer themselves the compassion, patience, and unconditional acceptance they had longed for. They were learning to show up for friends, partners, and children with the presence and care they had needed but not received. This was not about compensating for what they had lost, although overcompensation had occurred for some of them. It was about refusing to perpetuate the patterns they had inherited, modeling behavior characterized by emotional honesty, healthy boundaries, reciprocal care, and genuine connection. Daughters did not perfect these new behaviors and move on. They practiced them daily. They noticed when old patterns resurfaced — because they did resurface — but they remained committed to choosing differently. Healing was not a destination. It was a practice, a daily choice to prioritize wholeness over survival, connection over self-protection, growth over stagnation.

Community as a Site of Healing

While individual healing practices were essential, daughters also emphasized the critical role of community in their healing. For Black women, healing in isolation is difficult and often unsustainable. Healing in community with other Black women who understand, who have walked similar paths, and who can hold space for pain and celebrate growth, creates conditions for deeper, more resilient transformation.

Girlfriends, Sorors, and Fictive Kin

Many daughters described leaning heavily on their girlfriends. The women they had known for years, who knew their stories, who had witnessed their struggles, and loved them unconditionally. These friendships became safe havens where daughters could be fully themselves without judgment and process their maternal relationships without having to explain or justify their pain. For daughters who were members of Black sororities, their sorors provided similar support. The bonds formed in sisterhood organizations often ran deep, built on shared commitment to uplift and support one another. These women checked in regularly, offered encouragement, showed up in crisis, and celebrated victories. They reminded the Sagacious Seventeen that they were not alone and were loved. Some daughters also spoke of chosen family, people who were not biologically related, but who functioned as kin in the ways that mattered. These were the friends who became like sisters, the older women who provided mentorship and mothering, and the communities that offered belonging when biological families could not. Fictive kin filled gaps, provided models of healthy relating, and demonstrated that family is not just about blood but about care, commitment, and mutual support.

Safe Spaces to Be Seen

What these relationships offered was something daughters had often lacked in their maternal relationships: the experience of being fully seen and still loved. In their friendships and chosen family, daughters could share their struggles without fear of criticism, express anger without being told they were overreacting, and could cry without being shamed for weakness. Also, these were the relationships where they could celebrate achievements without worrying about being torn down. These soft places to land became mirrors that reflected daughters' worth. When your mother tells you that you are not enough, having friends who insist that you are more than enough can literally save your life. When your mother makes you feel invisible, having sisters who see you, name your gifts, and celebrate your existence creates a counter-narrative powerful enough to challenge internalized shame. Daughters described how these relationships allowed them to practice vulnerability and trust in ways that felt impossible with their mothers. They could take risks—sharing deeper pain, asking for support, being honest about their needs—and experience positive responses. Over time, these experiences rewired their beliefs about what relationships could be and their own worthiness of love and care.

Collective Healing

Beyond individual friendships, some daughters participated in or created spaces specifically for collective healing. This consisted of support groups for Black women, group counseling focused on maternal relationships, and online communities where Black daughters could share their stories and find solidarity. These spaces normalized experiences that once felt isolating, provided validation that individual therapy sometimes could not, and reminded daughters that their struggles were part of larger patterns requiring communal response. The importance of community in Black culture made these collective spaces particularly resonant. Healing in community honored African traditions of communal problem-solving and collective care. It resisted the individualistic approach common in Western therapy and self-help practices and instead recognized that healing happens in relationship and community.[15] For many daughters, the gift of collective healing spaces was not only support but also permitted them to stop carrying their stories alone.

Shandra described what it meant to finally speak what she had long kept hidden:

"… for a lot of years, I lived with a lot of shame, and I lived in silence where I didn't share what my childhood was like, what my mom was like, because I was embarrassed by having a mom that had mental health issues that people around town always whispered and laughed about because of her challenges. And then when I finally got my voice and started talking to other people, I realized I wasn't in this alone."

What Shandra found in her community was what silence had prevented: the experience of being known fully and not judged for it. When daughters like Shandra brought their hidden stories into shared space and were met with recognition rather than shame, something shifted. The story was no longer a source of isolation. It became a point of connection. The transformation from shame carried alone to pain held in community is one of the most powerful things collective healing spaces make possible.

Daughters also described how healing alongside other Black women created both accountability and inspiration. For Black women, when they see another Black woman doing the hard work of healing — breaking cycles, setting boundaries, and building healthier relationships—it makes their own feel more possible. Her courage becomes an invitation. Her progress becomes proof that change can happen. When a Black woman shares her story and watches other Black women nod in recognition, something shifts. She realizes she is not crazy, not alone, and not uniquely damaged. The shame that once isolated her begins to loosen its grip. What once felt like a private burden becomes a shared reality, held in community rather than carried in silence.

Breaking the Cycle

Daughters were explicit about their commitment to being cycle-breakers. Jen described a moment of reckoning that catalyzed her commitment to breaking cycles:

"I actually had to step back. I was like, sh*t, you're becoming your mother, you need to stop and take care of this and figure this out because if not, you're just going to perpetuate the cycle again."[16]

Jen's willingness to name what she saw in herself— patterns emerging that mirrored her mother—and immediately redirect toward healing demonstrates the vigilance and honesty cycle-breaking requires.

Shandra spoke even more directly about the consequences of unaddressed harm:

"…our parents do so much harm to us that we've become stunted adults, and we need to break these generational curses… so we don't raise another generation that is stunted emotionally."[17]

Shandra did not speak of these cycles with condemnation. She spoke of them with urgency. Shandra and the other daughters expressed the healing that they desired, not only for themselves but for the Black community as a whole. They want conversations about mental health to be normalized, and for therapy to be accessible and destigmatized. For the Sagacious Seventeen, ideally, they want the Black community to value emotional wellness alongside resilience, creating cycles of wholeness, instead of brokenness.

This cycle-breaking was not driven by shame. It was driven by love. It was love for themselves. Love for their children, their future children, their nieces, their girlfriends, and the generations of Black girls growing up behind them. Detaching from their mothers did not diminish the love that the Sagacious Seventeen have for Black women. In many cases, it intensified it. Mya expressed this devotion plainly:

"I love Black women… I want the very best for Black women!"[18]

Joy echoed this pride:

"I am very proud of my ethnicity. I'm proud to be a Black woman… very loud and boisterous about it!"[19]

Daughters' experiences fostered solidarity rather than alienation. Having endured maternal harm, they developed greater empathy for the burdens Black women carry — the invisible weight of generational trauma, societal pressure, and emotional survival. They do not want Black women to feel abandoned. They want Black women to rest, experience tenderness, and live beyond survival. They longed for a world where Black daughters are raised feeling cherished rather than criticized, protected rather than hardened, and secure rather than self-reliant out of necessity. They imagined a future where Black mothers show up with emotional presence, care, and tenderness. The daughters understood that creating such a future required them to do the healing work their mothers had not been given the space, support, or tools to do. In this way, their personal healing became inseparable from collective transformation within the Black community. They recognized that the behaviors they were addressing were not merely individual struggles but cultural patterns shaping countless Black families. By engaging in their own healing, they believed they were participating in a broader cultural shift, one that insists Black women deserve to heal, rest, prioritize their mental health, and build lives defined by peace rather than perpetual endurance. This vision gave their healing a deeper meaning. They were not healing for themselves alone. They were healing for the Black daughters who came before them and did not have the language, resources, or permission to heal. They were healing for the Black daughters who will come after them, who deserve to inherit wholeness rather than woundedness. They were healing for their families, for our communities, and for a future in which love — not survival alone — defines what it means to be mothered.

8

Mothers Are Human, Too

The Distance That Brings Clarity

If you have spent any time trying to understand mothers, to make sense of how they became who they became, this chapter is where that conceptualizing can begin. For fourteen out of seventeen daughters in this study, detachment eventually created the conditions under which understanding their mothers became possible.[1] The distance gave them something proximity had always prevented: The space to see their mothers not just as the sources of their pain, but as women with their own stories. Daughters began to realize that their mothers' behaviors were often rooted in their mothers' own unmet needs and unhealed trauma. This awareness did not make the pain less real. It did, though, provide context that helped daughters make sense of why their mothers had been unable to show up in the ways they needed.

The recognition of mothers' humanity was complex and often uncomfortable. It required daughters to hold multiple truths simultaneously. Their mothers had been wounded, and they inflicted wounds. Their mothers were shaped by experiences that limited their capacity, and they still made choices that harmed them. This both/and thinking, the capacity to see mothers as both victims of their own circumstances and perpetrators of harm, reflected the emotional maturity and nuance that many daughters developed through their healing journeys. For them, when it came to their reflections on their maternal relationships, compassion and accountability coexisted.[2]

Seeing Mothers as Wounded Daughters

One of the most profound shifts that occurred for many daughters was recognizing that their mother was also a daughter who was wounded.[3] The Sagacious Seventeen's mothers were daughters who carried unhealed trauma into their parenting, replicating inherited patterns because they were never given tools or support to do differently. Diana articulated this perspective succinctly:

"I don't wanna say she's a bad person, but just a traumatized individual."[4]

Diana's distinction — not bad, but traumatized — reflects a cognitive reframe that allowed her to see her mother's behavior as stemming from unresolved pain rather than inherent malice or moral failure. This reframe did not make what her mother did acceptable, but it made it comprehensible. Her mother was not cruel because she was evil. She was cruel because she was carrying wounds she had never healed.

Intergenerational Transmission of Trauma

Many daughters described being aware, to varying degrees, of the traumatic aspects of their mothers' upbringings.[5] They knew or suspected that their mothers had experienced abuse, neglect, poverty, or other forms of harm during childhood. They recognized patterns repeating across generations: mothers who had been emotionally unavailable because their own mothers had been emotionally unavailable, mothers who had been harsh and critical because they had been raised with harshness and criticism, and mothers who could not provide nurturing because they had never been nurtured. Shandra explained:

"I always had a challenging relationship because my mom has her own trauma background with her mother. In my mom's generation, the Silent Generation, they didn't really talk about a lot of things."[6]

Shandra's recognition that her mother belonged to a generation where emotional expression was suppressed, and trauma was not addressed, provided context for why her mother could not engage emotionally. It did not make Shandra's need for emotional connection less valid, but it helped her understand that her mother's limitations were not about Shandra's unworthiness.

Michelle offered a detailed account of intergenerational trauma in her family:

"So genetically, there's trauma. My grandmother was in an abusive relationship with her husband, who is my mother's father, and left him while she was pregnant with my mother. [My grandmother became] a single mom. And this was in the 70s... a single Black woman with two kids, that's not easy. She was doing it all by herself; she couldn't afford health insurance, dental insurance, and things like that, and was never dealing with her own trauma. My mom learned how to live in survival mode."[7]

Michelle's narrative traces the transmission of survival mode parenting across generations. Her grandmother, fleeing an abusive relationship and raising children alone without resources, had no capacity to address her own trauma. She simply survived. And that survival mode, characterized by focus on basic provision without emotional processing or healing, was what Michelle's mother learned and then replicated in raising Michelle. The pattern continued not because each generation chose it consciously but because each generation inherited it and lacked the tools or support to interrupt it.

Mothers' Relationships with Their Own Mothers

Several daughters reflected specifically on their mothers' relationships with their grandmothers, recognizing that those dynamics impacted how their moms understood and enacted motherhood.[8] In many cases, their mothers had strained, abusive, or no relationship with their grandmothers, and those relational templates informed how the Sagacious Seventeen was mothered. Some daughters described their mothers as having been the overlooked or neglected child. Charity explained:

"I think everything is a result of her mom passing at 8. One of her sisters took her in to get a check, and she was pretty much ignored in that household. She was, you know, the good kid, and she was the one who excelled academically. But the other children in that household weren't up to par with her, and they were given accolades, but she was ignored, and I think that has done a lifetime of destruction as it would for anybody."[9]

Charity's mother's childhood experience of being ignored likely contributed to her self-absorption in adulthood, including the ways she cultivated a non-reciprocal relationship with her daughter. On the surface, it can appear as though Charity's mother is not interested in hearing Charity's life, given their phone calls center on the mother, but it could also be a desperate attempt for Charity's mom to finally be seen and centered after a lifetime of invisibility.

Lisa also discussed her mother's experiences of feeling like the forgotten child:

"My grandmother left my grandfather and returned to Arkansas. When she did that, my great-grandmother, my grandmother's mother, said, 'Well, I can't take you and all your girls too. You can leave one girl'. My mother is the middle child and was the one who was left with my great-grandmother. She's always wondered why. She never knew why. My aunts would get to go places, dances, hang out, and go to the community center. And my mother didn't. Her grandmother didn't let her go anywhere. So, [that's where] a lot of [the tension between my mother and grandmother]".[10]

Similar to Charity's mother, Lisa's mom could have perceived that her interactions with Lisa were the only time she got to be seen, contributing to her self-centered tendencies.

Daughters' mothers not being primarily raised by their own grandmothers was a recurring pattern in the study. Brooklyn shared:

"My grandmother was not a good mom to my mom. [My mom will] even say my great-grandma was her mom. My grandma would say her kids didn't stop her life, but she was a young mom as well, and she was the baby [out of] her 11 brothers and sisters. One of my great aunts technically raised my mom. [My great-grandmother and great aunts worked and made sure [my mom and her siblings] had everything. My grandma never really had a career. My grandma was a party girl. She was out. She was skating. She was enjoying her life. And I honestly think she was the grandma that she was to us because her mom was the grandma that she was to her children."[11]

Between experiencing maternal absence and being raised in a family where it was customary for grandparents to be the primary caregivers, it was understandable how Brooklyn's mom became an absent mother. She was not intentional about being an engaged mother, nor was she expected to be one, as she was repeating the parenting practices that her own mother modeled.

Some daughters reflected on how their mothers experienced different forms of absence from their grandparents.[12] For example, although Hope's grandmother was her mother's primary caretaker, it did not prevent her mother from feeling neglected:

"My aunt was born premature… [causing her to have] learning disabilities… mental, physical, and anatomical issues. It was a lot… my aunt was a high needs child, and I think that my mother resents that. She says, 'Well, my mother wasn't there for me.' My mother will remind me of how parents are supposed to love equally."[13]

Hope's commentary is telling. It was clear that, despite her grandmother being physically present, Hope's mother felt that she was not emotionally attuned. She also did not feel loved by her mother, whose attention was focused on her younger sister. It is understandable as to why Hope's grandmother was actively involved with her youngest daughter. Concurrently, we must acknowledge that it came with a cost, in which Hope's mom was the one to pay.

Other daughters described mothers who had been parentified, forced to take on adult responsibilities as children, rather than being cared for themselves. Amina shared:

"My mom is very traumatized by my grandma. She talks about it with me because it helps fix our relationship… My grandmother was an alcoholic. My mother was the youngest and the last one at home. She bore the responsibility of making sure she ate, that their apartment wasn't on fire, and that my grandmother was just all around not dead."[14]

Caretaking for an adult with a substance use disorder and ensuring your parent does not die is a burden no child should carry. Parentification robs childhood, forcing kids into roles they are not developmentally equipped for, and teaches them that their own needs are irrelevant. When Amina's mother became a parent herself, she had no template for what healthy mothering looked like. She had only experienced being a caretaker, never being cared for. So, she replicated what she knew—expecting her daughter to function as a support system rather than offering herself as one.

Then, some daughters learned the drivers behind their mother's neurotic behavior. Diana's reflections provide insight into what drove her mother to the cult that she brought her to:

"My grandmother neglected my mom. She was left to be raised by my great-grandmother, who is a narcissist, after my grandfather was killed in a car crash. My mom was raped at 15 and also experienced domestic violence… my dad used to beat the brakes off of her. It was really insidious. And my mom ran to the church to the prophet or whatever. [The cult and the prophet] gave her comfort because all her questions were being "answered". Will I have a man? Will I get married this year? And he'll say, 'God say it. God speak it to me right now.' Just so he could tell her yes. It came down to the point where she would ask him if she should go to the store or stay home. She had no discernment, none whatsoever. Everything was completely codependent on this man."[15]

Diana's mother ran to a cult that she perceived to be safe. The "prophet's" behavior convinced her that she was secure, considered, and cared for in his presence, things that Diana's mom did not experience with her mother, great-grandmother, or Diana's father. Diana's mother felt that she was better off being in a cult than with her family. Perhaps Diana's mother thought Diana, too, would be better off in a cult than to be raised by her grandmother. And maybe, Diana's mother believed she was making the right choice for her daughter when she brought Diana alongside her to the cult.

These accounts reveal a painful truth. Many of the Sagacious Seventeen's mothers were themselves daughters who had never been properly mothered. They entered parenthood without models of tenderness, without having their own emotional needs met, and without the opportunity to heal the wounds of their childhoods. They were asked to give what they had never received. In the absence of intentional interruption—through therapy, meaningful support, or a conscious decision to parent differently—these inherited patterns continued. What was unhealed was repeated. What was unmet was passed forward. And so, across generations, the pain of inadequate mothering quietly reproduced itself.

The Factors That Constrained Mothers

Beyond the trauma and relational patterns inherited from their own childhoods, daughters recognized that their mothers had been constrained by multiple factors that limited their capacity to mother well.[16] These included suspected or known mental health issues, the demands of single motherhood and economic hardship, becoming mothers before developing a stable sense of self, and systemic factors that made survival-based parenting necessary.

Mental Health and Unresolved Trauma

Several daughters, particularly those with professional training in psychology or counseling, recognized that their mothers likely struggled with mental health issues that went undiagnosed and untreated. Cultural stigma around mental illness in Black communities meant that many mothers suffered without diagnosis, support, or treatment.[17] In many Black families, mental health struggles are not discussed openly — they are managed quietly, explained away as stress or spiritual warfare, or simply endured. Seeking therapy is often framed as a weakness, as airing family business, or as something "that's for crazy people". For some of the daughters' mothers, the expectation of strength resulted in mental health conditions that could have been treated — depression, anxiety, PTSD, personality disorders shaped by childhood trauma — and, instead, went unaddressed across entire lifetimes.

Jasmine, a psychologist, analyzed her mother's behavior through a clinical lens:

"My mother does not meet the criteria to [be diagnosed with Narcissistic Personality Disorder], but at the core of narcissistic traits is insecurity, and she has those traits."[18]

Jasmine's professional training gave her a framework for understanding her mother's behavior. The self-absorption, the constant need for validation, and the inability to empathize stemmed from a deep insecurity, not a deliberate cruelty. This understanding did not make her mother's behavior acceptable, but it reframed it from intentional harm to the manifestation of an untreated psychological struggle.

Jen also shared how she viewed her mother from a clinical lens:

"I started looking at my her, and her behavior, from a clinical standpoint, you know, doing a personality assessment or psychological assessment of [her] as a patient. So, separating myself from it, emotionally, and seeing it from a clinical perspective made it much easier for me to come to terms and realize [that her behavior had nothing to do with me] even though I was negatively affected by it."[19]

Jen's profession allowed her to understand her mother while also preventing her from internalizing the message that she was unlovable and unworthy of care, all without invalidating the pain she experienced as a child. Other daughters suspected depression, anxiety, unresolved PTSD from childhood trauma, or other conditions that shaped how their mothers functioned.[20] The lack of treatment meant these conditions influenced parenting in ways mothers may not have fully understood or been able to control. This does not absolve mothers of responsibility — adults are responsible for seeking help and managing their mental health — but it provides context for why some mothers were so emotionally dysregulated, unpredictable, or unable to attune to their daughters' needs.

Becoming Mothers Before Becoming Themselves

Several daughters recognized that their mothers had become parents before developing a stable sense of self.[21] Before knowing who they were, what they wanted, or what kind of mothers they hoped to be. Young motherhood and unplanned pregnancies meant that some women transitioned into the role of a parent without ever having the opportunity to explore their own identities, heal from their own wounds, or consciously make the choice to become a mom. Michelle reflected on how her mother's young, unplanned pregnancy shaped their relationship:

"I've always felt like a burden. One, because I was an accident. She had me at 21, so she didn't really have a young adulthood."[22]

Michelle's mother became a parent at an age when she should have been exploring who she was, what she wanted from life, and what brought her joy. Instead, she was responsible for another human being. The resentment Michelle sensed was not about Michelle as a person but about the loss of possibility. The young adulthood her mother never experienced, the dreams she never pursued, and the self she never discovered because motherhood came first.

Charity articulated a similar recognition:

"Because she was young, she never had the chance to learn about herself. She never had the chance to travel or be independent. She never really had the chance to say, 'This is my life, and this is how I want to live it.' She had a child before she was an adult."[23]

When someone becomes a mother before becoming an adult, they often lack the maturity and self-knowledge necessary for healthy parenting.[24] They are still figuring out who they are while being expected to guide someone else. This can pave the way for them to resent the child, seeing them as someone who represents their constrained choices, even though the child is not responsible for those limitations.

Moreover, Jada offered insight into mothers who had children for the wrong reasons and how those motivations set up relational dysfunction from the beginning:

"My mom was angry about being a mom. She was one of those people who want kids because they want unconditional love. And I think that's where she started off very, very wrong. I also think she went in with the mindset of, if I have these kids, this man is just gonna stay. Two factors that we all know just do not work since the beginning of time. Yet when you're in that situation, it doesn't click for you. And I think that's just her life. I don't think she ever wanted to be a mom."[25]

Jada's analysis reveals that her mother entered motherhood with expectations that children would meet her needs for love and a secure relationship, instead of understanding that mothers are supposed to meet children's needs. When those expectations were not fulfilled — when children required more than they gave, when the man left anyway — Jada's mother's anger and resentment were directed at her children. She blamed them for not being what she needed them to be, for not solving the problems she thought they would provide a solution for. Overall, these reflections reveal that daughters bear the consequences when mothers enter motherhood unprepared.

Empathy Without Reconciliation

Understanding why someone harmed you does not obligate you to maintain contact with them. Recognizing someone's humanity does not mean you have to sacrifice your own well-being to be in a relationship with them. Daughters were clear about this. They could see their mothers as wounded and traumatized, and still maintain firm boundaries. They could extend compassion while protecting themselves. They could wish their mothers well while refusing to have an intimate relationship with them. Moesha articulated this balance powerfully:

"You may not be able to resolve and deal with everything before you have kids but own it, and don't project that stuff onto your child and make your child be the punching bag of it."[26]

Moesha's statement acknowledges that perfect healing before parenting is unrealistic, as most people enter parenthood carrying unresolved wounds. But she insists on accountability: Own your limitations, take responsibility for your impact, and do not make your child bear the weight of your unhealed pain. Her empathy for the difficulty of parenting while wounded coexists with her demand that mothers take responsibility rather than projecting onto their children.

Throughout this study, a critical distinction has been carefully preserved: understanding why something happened is not the same as excusing that it happened. Explanation offers context. An excuse removes accountability. The Sagacious Seventeen worked to understand the forces that shaped their mothers, yet they refused to allow those explanations to absolve their mothers of responsibility for the harm they endured. Understanding allowed daughters to see that their pain was not a personal failure, not evidence of their unworthiness, but part of a larger pattern shaped by history, trauma, and unhealed wounds passed across generations. So, they chose not to flatten their mothers into simple categories of villain or victim. Instead, they came to see them as fully human, shaped by forces beyond their control, marked by their own suffering, and yet responsible for the pain they caused. In arriving at this understanding, daughters claimed something powerful: The right to compassion without self-erasure, understanding without denial, and accountability without hatred. They learned that acknowledging their mothers' humanity did not require abandoning their own.

9

Mothering to Break the Cycle

Mothering With Intention

Several daughters in this study demonstrate what becomes possible when a Black woman decides that the pain she inherited will not be the legacy she passes forward to her children, her nieces, her goddaughters, the younger women she mentors, or the version of herself she is still learning to nurture. Cycle-breaking is an act of intention, and the daughters raising children are the most visible practitioners of it, which brings us to the last exploration of RQ3. In previous chapters, we learned what detachment costs, but now it is time to focus on what it makes possible.

Among the seventeen daughters in this study, eight are mothers themselves. They inhabit a profound and complex reality, raising children while carrying the wounds of their own childhoods. They are parenting while still processing what it means to be inadequately parented and learning to give what they themselves were never given. What distinguishes these daughters is not simply that they are healing. It is that they are transforming their healing into intentional, conscious, and accountable mothering.[1] They are not waiting for healing to be complete before parenting differently. These daughters are breaking cycles in real time, in everyday interactions with their children. Each moment of attunement, each act of tenderness, and each effort to listen, protect, and nurture represents a deliberate departure from what they once experienced.

The mothers in this study described their parenting with a word that appeared repeatedly: intentional. Corrine succinctly stated:

"I am an intentional mother."[2]

This intentionality permeates everything — how they speak to their children, respond to misbehavior, create emotional safety, show affection, and how they deal with parenting mistakes. Nothing is automatic or unconscious. Everything is chosen. This level of intentionality can be overwhelming, though. It requires constant self-awareness, continuous self-correction, and the emotional bandwidth to be present even when triggered by stress or overstimulation. However, these mothers persist because they know what is at stake. They remember what it felt like to be children whose mothers were not intentional — who parented from reactivity, survival mode, or unhealed pain. These women are determined to make sure that their children will have different memories, different experiences, and different foundations.[3]

Being the Mother She Desired

Daughters described consciously embodying qualities they had longed for in their own mothers.[4] They were determined to give their children what had been withheld from them, to create the kind of maternal relationship they had wished for but never experienced.

Affection and Presence

For many of these daughters, demonstrating physical and verbal affection was central to how they parented differently.[5] They understood that their children needed to feel loved, not only in provision but in connection. Corrine explained:

"I tell them I love them with intention. Not just out of habit. I make sure I hug them, and I kiss them, and I make sure that I'm making memories with them."[6]

Corrine does not tell her children she loves them automatically or as a reflex. She does it with consciousness, ensuring that the words carry weight and meaning. She does not just go through the motions of affection. She creates it deliberately, making sure her children experience her love as real, consistent, and unconditional.

The creation of memories was also important to Corrine and other mothers.[7] They were not just focused on getting through each day or managing logistics. They were building relationships, creating moments of connection and joy that their children would carry forward. This stands in stark contrast to what many of them experienced — childhoods characterized by absence, including mothers who were physically there but emotionally gone. Mya articulated her commitment to being present with fierce clarity:

"My son is the only person I will never walk away from."[8]

Given Mya's experience of maternal inconsistency and the detachment she chose from her own mother, this statement is profound. She is doing what she can to ensure her son will never wonder if she believes he is worth showing up for. Mya also does not want her son to experience the abandonment that characterized her own childhood. Mya and the other daughters anchor their mothering in having an unwavering presence, being physically available, and emotionally attuned.

Michelle described her commitment to attachment:

"I was aware of attachment theory in [my daughter's early years]. I was uber attentive, and at this juncture, my therapist has confirmed she's a securely attached child, and that was my goal. To raise a securely attached child."[9]

Michelle's knowledge of attachment theory informed how she parented from day one. She understood that secure attachment—the foundation for healthy emotional development, successful relationships, and resilient coping—is built through consistent, responsive caregiving.[10] She was "uber attentive," not because she was helicoptering or anxious, but because she knew that attunement in early years creates internal working models of safety, trust, and worthiness that children carry for life.[11] Her daughter is experiencing what Michelle did not: The foundational belief that she is loved, that her needs matter, and that the world is a place where care is available. This is what it looks like to deliberately change the course for the next generation.

Creating Emotional Safety

Beyond affection and physical presence, these daughters spoke with deep conviction about creating environments where their children felt emotionally safe.[12] They described intentionally cultivating spaces where their children could speak freely, express their feelings, and advocate for themselves without fear of rejection or punishment. For many of these Black mothers, this commitment represented a radical departure from their own childhood experiences. They had been raised in homes where children's voices were minimized or silenced, where disagreement was interpreted as disrespect, and where emotional expression was often dismissed, ignored, or punished. To parent differently required them to challenge deeply internalized beliefs about authority, obedience, and emotional expression. Yet they were unwavering in their resolve to create something new.[13] They taught their children that feelings are valid and worthy of attention. They practiced vulnerability, allowing their children to witness that adults, too, experience complex emotions and that acknowledging them is a sign of strength rather than weakness. When their children expressed distress, they responded with validation rather than dismissal, and with curiosity rather than criticism. In doing so, they created relationships grounded not in fear, but in trust.

Emotional safety wasn't just about relationships; it also included the environments their children moved through every day. These daughters were deeply protective of their children's well-being. They were intentional about who had access to their children, what messages their children absorbed about their worth, and what environments they were permitted to enter.[14] Their personal experience taught them that childhood innocence and emotional security are fragile, and wounds inflicted in early life can echo across decades. Their vigilance did not reflect control, but a profound desire to shield their children from harms they themselves were never protected from.

Unconditional Love

At the core of their mothering was an unwavering commitment to loving their children unconditionally.[15] This love was not contingent upon performance, achievement, or obedience. It was not something their children had to earn. It existed simply because their children existed. For many of these daughters, this was a stark difference from their own experiences of maternal love, which had often been conditional, granted in response to good behavior, academic success, or their ability to meet their mothers' emotional needs. Determined to break this pattern, they made their love visible and unmistakable. They told their children they were loved. They demonstrated through consistent words and actions that their children's worth was inherent and unchanging.

Loving unconditionally, however, required significant internal work. It demanded that these

daughters regulate their responses so they could
parent from intention rather than from unresolved
pain. They learned to pause rather than react, to
respond with care rather than projection, and to
ensure their children were never made responsible
for their emotional well-being or sense of
fulfillment. This commitment required ongoing
healing. It meant refusing to use their children as
emotional confidants, resisting the pull to seek
validation through them, and dismantling patterns
that had once defined their own upbringing. In
choosing to love differently, they created relational
models that had never been modeled for them, and
they built new templates for connection from the
ground up. In doing so, these daughters gave their
children what they themselves had longed for: A
secure foundation of love, affirmation, and
belonging. They offered their children the
emotional stability and sense of worth that many of
them are still striving to cultivate within
themselves as adults. Their mothering, therefore,
was not simply an act of care but an act of
profound generational transformation.

Course Corrective Mothering: Taking Accountability

Despite their best intentions and consistent
effort, daughters acknowledged that they were not
perfect parents. There were moments when they
found themselves parenting in ways that mirrored
their own mothers.[16] However, what they did when
they recognized these patterns was transformative.
They took accountability, repaired their children,
and committed to doing better.

Recognizing the Harmful Patterns

A few daughters described moments of painful recognition, seeing themselves act in ways that reminded them of their mothers.[17] They noticed patterns emerging that they had sworn they would never repeat. Jada shared her experience:

"Becoming a single mom forced me to take a look in the mirror. I noticed how similar I was beginning to parent my son. Most of it was out of anger and frustration. My siblings had to tell me that I was wild and out of control. They were like, 'You're angry. I get that you're a single mom. I get that you didn't think it was going to happen to you, but it's out of control.' I was very angry about my situation, and I noticed I was acting like my mom because she was angry about being a mom. So, I had to take a step back and lean into what I knew as I was in school for counseling."[18]

Jada's reflection reveals several profound insights about accountability, self-awareness, and the courage required to parent differently. First, she confronted a painful truth. She recognized that she was parenting from anger and frustration, reproducing patterns she herself had endured. This level of honesty required her to look directly at behaviors that were difficult to acknowledge. Second, she remained open to feedback from her siblings, choosing humility over defensiveness. Rather than dismissing their concerns or protecting her ego, she allowed herself to be confronted. This willingness to listen reflects a deep commitment to growth and to becoming a different kind of parent. Third, she made a critical connection between her behavior and her mother's, recognizing the emotional parallel between her anger about single motherhood and her mother's anger about motherhood. In naming this connection, she disrupted the unconscious transmission of pain across generations. She saw the cycle clearly and chose not to continue it. Finally, she intentionally intervened in the pattern, drawing on her professional training in counseling to regulate her emotions and adopt different parenting practices. Her knowledge became a tool for transformation, allowing her to respond with intention rather than react from unresolved wounds.

This kind of self-awareness and willingness to be challenged is both rare, particularly for Black parents, and deeply courageous. Many parents, when confronted with their harmful behaviors, protect themselves through denial, justification, or resistance. Jada chose a more difficult path. She listened. She reflected. She accepted responsibility. And she changed course. Her story demonstrates what true accountability looks like. It is not perfection or the absence of mistakes, but the willingness to see oneself clearly, acknowledge harm, and engage in the difficult, ongoing work of change. In choosing accountability, Jada interrupted a generational pattern and created the possibility of a different future for her child.

Repair as Love

When these daughters recognized that they had acted in ways that hurt or failed their children, they did something their own mothers rarely or never did. They apologized. Daughters took responsibility for their impact and worked to repair the relationship with their children. Destiny described a moment when she found herself projecting her own pain onto her son:

"I texted him, and I was bawling when I sent the message, [and said, 'I'm sorry, Damian. I know what it feels like to not be heard.' I found myself pouring out what I've been trying to avoid onto him. And once I realized it, it broke me, because I know what it feels like."[19]

Destiny's apology is significant. She recognized that she was doing to her son what had been done to her. The recognition "broke" her because she knows intimately how damaging that experience is. Instead of choosing to minimize what she had done or expecting her son to get over it, she apologized. Her apology also modeled something essential for her son: that adults make mistakes, mistakes can be addressed, and relationships can survive conflict if people are willing to take responsibility. The willingness to apologize and repair is what makes these daughters different from Black mothers of previous generations. Their own mothers, when confronted about harm they caused, typically responded with defensiveness, deflection, or self-pity.[20] They made their daughters comfort them, reassure them, or simply suppress their hurt. These daughters are doing the opposite. They are modeling that accountability is an expression of love that does not diminish authority but strengthens relationships.

Continuous Self-Work

Course correction was not a one-time event for these daughters. It was an ongoing practice. Daughters recognized that parenting while healing from their own childhood wounds meant they would sometimes slip or have a need to pause and recalibrate. Still, they remained committed to the work. They stayed in therapy. They read books on parenting. They sought support from friends, partners, or other mothers who could offer perspective and encouragement. Some even prayed, journaled, and reflected. Overall, they did whatever was necessary to ensure that their children did not bear the weight of their unhealed pain. These daughters demonstrated humility and the understanding that love requires ongoing effort and intentionality. They illustrate how breaking cycles does not mean never making mistakes, rather it requires recognizing them, taking accountability, repairing with children, and committing to doing better. In doing this work, these daughters were giving their children something invaluable: The experience of being parented by someone who takes responsibility, repairs ruptures, and loves them enough to keep growing.

Protecting the Next Generation

For the daughters who maintained some level of contact with their own mothers, a complex challenge arose. They had to learn how to manage the grandmother-grandchild relationship in ways that allowed connection while protecting children from the harm they themselves had experienced.[21]

Daughters had to be vigilant, strategic, and willing to enforce boundaries that their own mothers often did not respect or understand.

Setting Firm Boundaries

Some daughters described having explicit conversations with their mothers about what would not be tolerated in interactions with grandchildren. Shandra recounted such a conversation:

"When my daughter was little, and my mom wanted to spend time getting to know her, I let my mom know that none of her past behaviors were acceptable. If I feel, see, or sense in any way that she was treating my daughter in the same way she treated my siblings and me, that she would have no contact with her granddaughter."[22]

Shandra's boundary was clear and non-negotiable. She did not leave room for ambiguity or assume her mother would naturally behave differently with her grandchild. She explicitly stated that the behaviors she experienced—the abuse, criticism, and emotional unavailability—were unacceptable and would result in complete cutoff from her granddaughter if they occurred. Shandra prioritized her daughter's safety over her mother's feelings. She understood that her primary responsibility was to protect her child, not to manage her mother's emotions or maintain appearances. The enforcement of boundaries was equally important as the setting of them.

Jada described her approach:

"I allow contact [between my son and my mother], but if it gets disrespectful, if she says something I don't like, I immediately say, 'You're not gonna talk to your grandma unless I'm around… I keep a close eye on the relationship."[23]

Jada's supervision of her son's relationship with her mother reflects active, ongoing vigilance. She does not simply set a boundary and hope for the best. She monitors interactions, pays attention to what her mother says, how her son responds, and intervenes immediately if her mother crosses lines. Her son does not have unsupervised access to his grandmother because Jada knows from experience that her mother cannot be trusted to behave appropriately without oversight. These daughters were not willing to gamble with their children's well-being because they knew what that would cost.

The Decision for No Contact

While some daughters permitted contact, even if it was limited or supervised, between their children and mothers, it is important to acknowledge that this was not the only approach. Some daughters explained that their children did not have contact with their mothers. They determined that supervised interaction posed too much risk or that their mothers' behavior was so harmful that no relationship was safe with them. These daughters understood what their choice meant. Their children would grow up without knowing their grandmothers, family gatherings would be complicated or impossible, and they would be judged by extended family or community for "depriving" their children of grandparents. They made the choice anyway because they prioritized their children's safety and well-being above all else.

Whether mothers allowed non-supervised contact, supervised contact, or chose complete separation, what united them was the commitment to protecting the next generation. They were ensuring that the cycles of harm they experienced would not be transmitted to their children. Daughters became the protectors they had wished their mothers would be.[24] The pain they had endured would not be wasted; it would become the foundation for a different kind of mothering.

Preparing to Break Cycles: Aspiring Mothers

Not all daughters in this study were mothers, yet several expressed a deep desire to become one in the future. For these aspiring mothers, the commitment to breaking cycles took on a particularly intentional form. They chose to heal now — before motherhood — so that they could one day parent from wholeness rather than from their wounds.[25] These daughters recognized that entering motherhood without addressing their own trauma would risk reproducing the very patterns they longed to end. They did not want to confront their anger only after it had touched their children, nor did they want to one day apologize for projecting unhealed pain onto the next generation. Instead, they committed to doing the difficult work in advance, striving to ensure that their children would be born into families where healing was already underway.

This proactive approach reflected wisdom and self-awareness. These daughters understood that love alone does not undo trauma, and that good intentions cannot compensate for unprocessed pain. They believed that children deserve mothers who are physically present and emotionally attuned, not mothers who unknowingly use their children to fill emotional voids or to resolve wounds inherited from previous generations. Their commitment to healing was therefore an act of protection, a deliberate refusal to allow inherited harm to shape the lives of children not yet born. In choosing this path, these women were interrupting generational cycles before those cycles had the opportunity to take hold. Like the daughters who were already mothers, they recognized that breaking cycles requires deliberate effort, conscious choice, and sustained emotional labor. Their healing was not merely personal preparation; it was an act of responsibility toward the future.

The Cycle Ends Here

The daughters who are mothers have undertaken work that cannot be glossed over, minimized, or taken for granted. What they are doing demands careful acknowledgment. They are confronting patterns of harm that have persisted across generations and choosing to become something different. They are becoming the models for the kind of motherhood they themselves never experienced. They are giving their children what many of them are still learning to give themselves: unconditional love, emotional safety, consistent presence, and the unwavering assurance that their worth is inherent. In doing so, they are reshaping what motherhood looks like within their families and creating new relational possibilities for future generations. This work is not easy. Parenting while healing, giving what you never received, managing relationships with your own mother while protecting your children, and remaining accountable when old patterns resurface demands extraordinary emotional labor. It requires sustained self-awareness, discipline, vulnerability, and courage. These mothers are not perfect, but they are intentional. They are not flawless, but they are committed. And their commitment is what makes transformation possible.

It would be remiss to overlook what the children being raised by these daughters are receiving. They get to experience being parented by Black women who are breaking cycles in real time. They are watching their mothers make mistakes and take responsibility. These are the lessons that create secure attachment and lay the foundations for healthy relationships across the lifespan. These daughters are not just parenting their children. They are shaping future generations, creating ripple effects that will extend far beyond their individual families. The healing they are doing, the cycles they are breaking, and the love they are modeling—all of this will be carried forward by their children, who will in turn have different templates for what Black families can be. The daughters' children are growing up knowing they are loved, simply because they exist. They are growing up with Black mothers who see them, hear them, and cherish them. This is triumph and

transformation. The daughters' parenting approach
consists of radical acts of love that interrupt cycles
of harm. These daughters are writing different
narratives for their Black children, ones full of
safety, belonging, and unconditional acceptance.
These stories will shape not just individual lives
but entire lineages, changing the trajectory of Black
families for generations to come.

IV

What God Says

10

The Dichotomy of Faith

The Church as Cornerstone

For generations, the church has stood as the spiritual and cultural heartbeat of the Black community. [1] Born in the crucible of slavery, the Black church emerged as far more than a place of Sunday morning service; It became a sacred refuge—a space where hope could be nurtured in the face of despair, where dignity could be affirmed in a society committed to denying it, and where faith became a means of survival.[2] Across generations, the church has functioned as a sanctuary and shelter, and demonstrates resistance and restoration, offering spiritual grounding alongside social support, political mobilization, and communal care.[3] It has been the place where suffering found language, where struggle found meaning, and where generations of Black families sought healing for wounds inflicted by an unjust world.[4]

Today, the Black church continues to hold influence within the Black community, serving as a pillar of strength for the collective. Yet for all its power as a communal institution, the church also exists in tension with deeply personal experiences of pain that unfold within Black families, particularly in relationships between Black mothers and their daughters. When mothers who publicly embody faith privately enact harm, daughters experience a rupture that extends beyond the maternal relationship into their spiritual lives. They must reconcile the image of their mothers as devoted women of God—sometimes celebrated within church communities and positioned as spiritual mothers to others—with their lived reality of emotional, psychological, or physical harm. This dissonance produces a profound spiritual crisis. Daughters are left to wrestle not only with maternal betrayal but also with questions about faith itself. They navigate church cultures that often emphasize family loyalty, maternal honor, and forgiveness while leaving little room for truth-telling about harm, accountability, or personal safety. In such contexts, daughters must determine how to hold onto their faith while confronting the painful contradiction between what was preached and what was lived.

It is necessary to explore the complex intersection of faith, family, and harm because daughters, within and beyond this study, were raised by mothers who identified as Christian yet embodied behaviors that contradicted the love of Christ. Furthermore, it is important to discuss how church communities often reinforce harmful cultural expectations, deepen daughters' silence, or complicate their healing. We must also consider the theological and spiritual questions that emerged when the primary earthly representation of God's love—their mothers—failed them so profoundly. At the same time, harboring issues without presenting solutions is not fruitful. So, this chapter moves towards restoration. It offers clarity about what Scripture actually requires of mothers and daughters, confronts the spiritual realities underlying mother–daughter conflict, and points toward the hope found in God's promise of belonging and adoption for daughters who were not nurtured by their earthly mothers.

When Christian Mothers Don't Reflect Christ

Several daughters in the study were raised in homes where church attendance was non-negotiable, and faith was presented as central to family life.[5] Jada explained:

"… when I wanted to do things as a teenager, my mom was like, 'No, this is a Christian household, and we do things the right way. All you need to do is go to school, get your education, and go to church.'"

Jada's statement gave me pause. In response, I asked her:

"Did your mom reflect biblical values in the way Jesus taught us to treat people?"

Jada succinctly replied:

"No, she did not."

To the outside observer, some of the Sagacious Seventeens' mothers exemplified Christian devotion. But behind closed doors, or not at all, their treatment of their daughters told a different story. This disconnect between public faith and private behavior created confusion for daughters. The primary woman in their lives — the one who

should have been their first teacher of God's love—
demonstrated something else entirely. This
discrepancy was not merely disappointing. It was
disorienting, calling into question everything
daughters had been taught about what it meant to
follow Christ.

Diana's experience illustrates an extreme
manifestation of this dynamic.[6] Her mother
brought her into a cult led by a man who claimed
to be a prophet with a direct connection to God. For
twenty years, Diana endured what she described as
"pure hell".[7] When Diana finally left, she had to
leave her mother behind, still entrenched in the
deception. Diana's story is not representative of all
participants' experiences, but it reveals a truth that
resonated across many accounts. When mothers
use faith as a weapon or a shield rather than as a
source of godly love, they harm their daughters
relationally, distorting their daughters'
understanding of who God is.

Within and outside of this research, daughters
describe how spiritual language was used in ways
that deepened their wounds rather than healed
them, alluding to the ways their mothers, family
members, and church communities invoked God's
name to justify harmful behavior, demand
obedience, or silence daughters' pain. Their appeals
to faith were often used to discourage
confrontation, suppress emotions, or frame
daughters' suffering as a test of character rather
than a call for accountability. A few of the
Sagacious Seventeen reflected on how certain
church structures made accountability difficult,

allowing harmful patterns to persist unchecked. In some cases, mothers participated in religious environments where personal relationships with spiritual leaders were limited and meaningful discipleship was absent. Without spaces for correction, guidance, or accountability, destructive behaviors remained unchallenged. Michelle described this reality plainly:

"My mom has created a life void of accountability. She goes to a megachurch where nobody can check her. She does not have a pastor to hold her accountable."

Additionally, Bible verses about honoring and obeying parents were frequently invoked in daughters' narratives.[8] Yet when these biblical teachings were removed from their fuller context and applied without pastoral care, they often became tools of witchcraft—used to justify manipulation, enforce dominance, and silence daughters' pain.

The spiritual consequences of this experience run deep. When a mother claims to represent Jesus Christ yet relates to her daughter with coldness, criticism, or cruelty, the daughter's understanding of Jesus Himself can become distorted. She may begin to wonder whether the Lord, too, is distant, harsh, or unloving. If the person who gave her life cannot embody the love of Christ toward her, what does this suggest about the God she worships? In this way, maternal harm not only wounds the heart, but it can also fracture faith, reshaping how daughters perceive divine love, care, and presence.

The Conflation: When God Is Perceived As Your
Mother

For many daughters, the mother becomes the
first lens through which they understand divine
love. When that lens is distorted, so too is their
perception of God. If a mother's love felt
conditional — granted only when a daughter
performed well, complied without question, or met
constantly shifting expectations — then God's love
may also be perceived as something to be earned
rather than freely given. If a mother were
emotionally distant or inaccessible, God may feel
distant and unreachable. If a mother is quick to
criticize and slow to affirm, daughters may come to
expect judgment rather than compassion from their
Heavenly Father. In this way, maternal harm does
not remain confined to the relational sphere; it
reshapes spiritual understanding. Thus, the God
who daughters encounter becomes filtered through
the wounds inflicted by the very person who
taught them who God was supposed to be.

The Bible's Witness to Mother Wounds

The study's biblical integration highlights that
when mothers fail to reflect the parental nature of
God — His love, protection, nurturance, and
guidance — daughters are deprived not only of
maternal care but of a living expression of God's
character in their own lives. More than a personal
failure, this misrepresentation grieves God because
it distorts who He is. God designed the parent-
child relationship to embody His love and care.[9]
When mothers fall short of this sacred calling,
daughters experience a double loss: the absence of

the nurture they deserved and a fractured understanding of divine truth.

God Accounts for the Human Experience

Before addressing what Scripture teaches about mothers' and daughters' responsibilities to one another, it is essential to acknowledge a foundational biblical reality. God is not surprised by the existence of harmful mothers. Scripture does not present an idealized vision of motherhood where every woman naturally embodies nurturing care and godly love. Instead, the Bible accounts for the full range of human experience—including mothers who are physically absent, emotionally unavailable, or spiritually destructive—and it offers both lament and hope for daughters who have been failed.

The Old Testament provides multiple accounts of daughters whose mothers were either physically or emotionally absent during critical moments of need. Lot's wife offers one of the starkest examples—a mother who literally disappeared before her daughters' eyes— after deliberately disobeying God's command not to look back at Sodom as it was being destroyed.[10] Her absence left her daughters motherless, and though Scripture does not detail how her absence affected them, the narrative immediately following suggests dysfunction. Both daughters, believing they were the last people on earth, got their father drunk and committed incest with him—each conceiving a child[11] The sons born from this incest became the fathers of two nations, the Ammonites and Moabites, who would become perpetual adversaries of Israel.[12] While the text does not draw a direct causal link between their mother's death and their choices, the proximity is impossible to ignore. Although we do not know what would have been different if Lot's wife obeyed, we learn that when mothers are absent, daughters are left to navigate trauma without maternal guidance. And trauma, unprocessed and unwitnessed, leads people to make choices they might never have made if someone had been there to hold their pain with them.

Dinah's story offers another sobering example, one that reveals the devastating silence that can occur when a mother is too consumed by her own pain to protect her daughter. After Dinah was raped by Shechem, her mother, Leah, is notably absent from the narrative.[13] There is no account of Leah running to her daughter. No mention of her holding Dinah as she wept. Instead, Dinah's brothers responded with rage and violence.[14] We do not know what Leah was doing after her assault, but the information that we do have about Leah gives context. Leah was the unloved wife that Jacob never wanted.[15] She was the one who spent her entire marriage trying to earn the affection of a man whose heart belonged to her sister Rachel. Each pregnancy Leah had was an attempt to secure love that would never come.[16] Each son was a bid for validation from a man who could not see her. With this in mind, it is plausible that Leah lacked the emotional capacity to tend to her daughter because she was fixated on her own unmet need — her desperation for a husband who remained emotionally unavailable. Whether due to her own unhealed wounds or her consuming preoccupation with her marital struggles, Leah was not present for Dinah in the way a mother should be. And Dinah was left to navigate the aftermath without the one person who should have wrapped her in safety. The Scripture does not tell us what became of Dinah after that day. But the silence suggests a girl left alone with her pain, a daughter whose mother could not mother her when she needed it most.

Tamar's experience is perhaps the most explicit and most devastating account of maternal absence in the aftermath of sexual violence. After being raped by her half-brother Amnon—who lured her into his room under the pretense of being sick, then overpowered her despite her pleas—Tamar's life was shattered.[17] And in her shattering, she was met with a father's impotent rage and a mother's complete absence. King David, when he heard what Amnon had done to his daughter, became furious.[18] But fury without action is abandonment. David did nothing. And Tamar's mother, Maacah? She is absent from the narrative. Instead, it was Tamar's brother Absalom who became her protector, and eventually her avenger.[19]

Tamar's grief is visceral in the text. Scripture records that she put dust on her head, tore the ornate robe that marked her as a virgin princess, put her hand on her head, and went away crying out.[20] This was not her quietly weeping. She was wailing. This was a daughter whose body had been violated, whose trust had been shattered, whose future had been stolen (because in that culture, a woman who had been raped was considered unmarriageable, her life effectively over). She was crying out for someone—anyone—to see her pain, to acknowledge what had been done to her, to tell her she was not alone. The Bible does not state where her mother was, and if she was absent, we do not know why. Perhaps Maacah was one of David's many wives and lacked the social power to confront the king or his favored son. Maybe she was too consumed with navigating the political intrigue of a polygamous household to tend to her daughter's trauma. It is possible she did not know how to mother a daughter through sexual violence. Or she could have been emotionally unavailable in ways that predated Tamar's assault, and her absence in this moment was simply the most visible manifestation of a lifelong pattern. Tamar's story is not ancient history. It is a mirror held up to every daughter who has experienced harm and found her mother missing in the aftermath, who needed protection and received silence, who cried out and heard nothing in return.

These biblical accounts are not presented to vilify mothers or to suggest that maternal absence or failure is acceptable. Rather, they reveal that Scripture honestly acknowledges a painful reality: some mothers fail their daughters—through disobedience, emotional incapacity, or neglect. God does not minimize these experiences, ignore them, or ask daughters to deny their reality. Instead, He makes space for them within the biblical narrative, providing language for lament, validation for their pain, and pathways toward healing and restoration.

For some Black daughters in this study, and around the world, this truth matters deeply. Their experiences of maternal harm are not outside the scope of biblical truth. They are seen. They are known. They are held within the compassionate gaze of God. He does not require them to pretend their mothers' failures did not occur, nor does He ask them to silence the wounds those failures created. God sees their suffering, grieves with them in their pain, and meets them in the place where loss and longing coexist.

What the Bible Says About Mothers and Daughters

Before we walk through what Scripture actually teaches, I want to acknowledge that these passages have been used against daughters. Many have sat in a pew or across from a family member and heard these verses quoted as reasons to endure harm, stay silent, or return to a relationship that was costing them everything. What follows is not that. This is an attempt to return these Scriptures to their actual meaning — the one that holds both mothers and daughters accountable, and that has never required a daughter to sacrifice herself in the name of honoring someone who was harming her.

God's Expectations for Mothers

The Bible is clear that mothers have a divine responsibility to care for their children in ways that reflect God's character. Psalm 127:3 declares:

"Don't you see that children are God's best gift? The fruit of the womb his generous legacy?" (MSG)[21]

Children are not possessions that mothers own. Children are gifts entrusted to mothers by God, who retains ownership and expects mothers to faithful stewardship of the lives placed in their care. This stewardship includes meeting children's basic needs. Paul writes in 1 Timothy 5:8:

"Anyone who neglects to care for family members in need repudiates the faith. That's worse than refusing to believe in the first place." (MSG)[22]

Mothers are called to provide for their daughters, not just materially, but emotionally, spiritually, and relationally. Neglect is not a minor failing. It is a rejection of the Christian faith itself. Moreover, mothers are explicitly instructed not to provoke their children. Ephesians 6:4 states:

"Fathers, do not provoke your children to anger [do not exasperate them to the point of resentment with demands that are trivial or unreasonable or humiliating or abusive; nor by showing favoritism or indifference to any of them], but bring them up [tenderly, with lovingkindness] in the discipline and instruction of the Lord." (AMP)[23]

Colossians 3:21 reiterates:

"Fathers, do not provoke or irritate or exasperate your children… so they will not lose heart and become discouraged or unmotivated [with their spirits broken]." (AMP)[24]

Though these verses address fathers specifically, the principle applies to mothers as well. God does not give one parent permission to provoke, abuse, or demoralize while holding the other parent accountable. Both fathers and mothers are called to raise their children with tenderness, lovingkindness, and in ways that do not break their spirits.

Some mothers fail to meet these biblical standards. Instead of providing emotional safety and nurturance, many were sources of criticism, control, and harm. Instead of tenderly guiding their daughters, they provoked them through harsh treatment, neglect, emotional abuse, and the weaponization of Scripture to demand compliance. These behaviors are not aligned with God's design for motherhood. In fact, they represent a departure from what He calls mothers to be.

God's Expectations for Daughters

Scripture also sets clear expectations for daughters regarding their mothers. Exodus 20:12 commands:

"Honor your father and mother. Then you will live a long, full life in the land the Lord your God is giving you" (MSG)[25]

The Hebrew word for "honor" — kabod — means to treat someone with weight, significance, and glory.[26] It is not a light command. These verses establish that daughters have a responsibility to respect and honor their mothers as part of their obedience to God. And importantly, God does not make concessions for daughters who have been neglected, abandoned, or harmed. Daughters are still called to honor their mothers.

Additionally, Ephesians 6:1 charges daughters to obey their mothers:

"Children, obey your parents in the Lord [that is, accept their guidance and discipline as His representatives], for this is right." (AMP)[27]

Colossians 3:20 echoes:

"Children, obey your parents [as God's representatives] in all things, for this [attitude of respect and obedience] is well-pleasing to the Lord." (AMP)[28]

It is critical to note that these verses imply that mothers are instructing their daughters in ways that align with God's commands and draw them closer to Him. Further, obedience does not equate to unconditional compliance with harmful demands. It does not mean accepting abuse. It does not require you to silence your pain or pretend harm did not happen. And one Bible verse does not counter or negate another. Both mothers and daughters have responsibilities. You cannot demand that daughters honor mothers who are actively provoking them while ignoring the command that mothers not provoke in the first place.

The Call to Forgive

The Bible explicitly addresses forgiveness, and this is where many daughters feel spiritually trapped. Matthew 18:21-22 records Peter asking:

"Lord, how many times will my brother sin against me and I forgive him and let it go? Up to seven times?"

Jesus responds:

"I tell you, not seven times, but seventy-seven times." (NIV)[29]

Forgiveness is not a one-time event but an ongoing posture of the heart, and Christians are expected to forgive for each wrongdoing, regardless of how often it occurs. Forgiveness is not the same as reconciliation, though. Forgiveness is about releasing the offense to God, choosing not to carry the burden of bitterness, and trusting that He will bring justice in His time and His way. It does not mean pretending the harm did not happen. It does not mean re-entering an unsafe relationship. It does not mean allowing the cycle of pain to continue. Daughters can forgive their mothers and still maintain boundaries. This is perhaps the most important clarification this chapter offers, so it bears repeating plainly. Honoring your mother does not mean pretending she did not harm you. It does not mean re-entering a relationship that continues to wound you. It does not mean suppressing the truth of your experience to preserve her reputation or the appearance of family unity. Honor, in its biblical meaning, is about how you carry yourself in relation to your mother, not what you are required to endure from her. When mothers fail to meet God's expectations, daughters are not required to absorb the consequences indefinitely.

The Spiritual Battle Behind the Relational Wound

The study's biblical integration raised a point that many daughters have never considered or are not privy to: Strained mother-daughter relationships are not merely emotional or psychological issues. They are spiritual battles. Genesis 3:15 records God's decree to the serpent after the fall:

"And I will put enmity (open hostility) between you and the woman, and between your seed (offspring) and her Seed; He shall [fatally] bruise your head, And you shall [only] bruise His heel." (AMP)[30]

The enemy, satan (whose name is intentionally not capitalized, as he is not worthy of honor, reverence, or distinction), has long waged war against women because God chose a woman to bring forth the Seed — Jesus Christ — who has already defeated him. The attacks on women, and particularly on the relationship between mothers and daughters, are not random. They are strategic. When the bond between a mother and her daughter is fractured, the damage reaches far beyond the individuals involved. Pain is inflicted on both. The generational transmission of faith, wisdom, and emotional wholeness is disrupted. Lineages become marked by the mother wound, where daughters grow up questioning their worth, doubting God's love, and unknowingly repeating the very relational patterns that wounded them. By sowing division where nurture, safety, and unity should exist, the enemy perpetuates cycles of harm that echo across generations.

This reality does justify harmful behavior. Human beings are given free will, and mothers remain responsible for their choices. But it does offer a broader lens for understanding the depth and complexity of the pain. The breakdown of the mother-daughter relationship is not merely a family conflict; it is a spiritual assault on womanhood, identity, generational continuity, and on daughters' ability to know and trust God. Recognizing this spiritual dimension shifts the focus. Rather than simply demonizing mothers, it invites us to see the larger forces at work. Mothers may have wounded their daughters, and they are often wounded themselves. They may have perpetuated generational harm, and they are also products of it. The enemy's aim is clear: Ensure that each generation experiences a strained maternal relationship, creating a legacy of pain. But God's intention is altogether different.

The Hope: God as the Adopting Father

Here is the most beautiful truth in all of Scripture for daughters who have been failed by their mothers: God always planned to adopt them. Ephesians 1:5 says:

"He predestined and lovingly planned for us to be adopted to Himself as [His own] children through Jesus Christ, in accordance with the kind intention and good pleasure of His will." (AMP)[31]

Long before daughters were born, before their mother's failures that caused pain, God decided that they would be His daughters. Not because of anything they did or did not do. Not because they earned it or deserved it. But because it pleased Him. Romans 8:15-16 affirms:

"For you have not received a spirit of slavery leading again to fear [of God's judgment], but you have received the Spirit of adoption as sons [the Spirit producing sonship] by which we [joyfully] cry, "Abba! Father!" (AMP)[32]

The Spirit of adoption is not a consolation prize for daughters whose earthly mothers failed them. It is the inheritance of every Believer, the assurance that you belong to God as He calls you His own. His adoption makes your identity secure in Him. Furthermore, Psalm 27:10 states:

"Although my father and my mother have abandoned me, Yet the Lord will take me up [adopt me as His child]" (AMP)[33]

Even if your mother abandoned you — physically, emotionally, or both — God will not. He sees the daughters who were left motherless, whether by death or a broken relationship, and He steps into that void.

This is the lived reality that daughters experience as they detach from their mothers and start the work of healing. Detachment creates a space for daughters to encounter God apart from their mothers' distortions. To hear His voice without her interference. To receive His love without her conditions. To discover that He is nothing like their mothers. God's love is not conditional, and His adoption is irrevocable. Unlike earthly mothers who may withdraw their affection

when daughters disappoint them, God's
commitment to them, to us, is eternal.[34] For
daughters who have spent their lives longing for a
mother's love they never received, this is the balm.
God offers what your mother could not. He gives
the love, safety, and belonging that you were
created to experience. And through spiritual
adoption, He gives you access to a divine model of
care that some earthly maternal relationships
cannot.

Moving Forward

Being raised by a Christian mother who did not
embody Christ creates damage that is layered —
relational and spiritual, personal and theological —
and it cannot be undone in a single conversation or
a single chapter. But healing is possible. Not
because the harm was not real, but because the God
who allowed it to be recorded in the Bible is the
same God who can make us whole. Moreover,
Scripture declares the truth about our identity. The
wounds caused by earthly mothers do not define
women in the Christian faith. They are God's
daughters, adopted, beloved, and secure in a love
that mothers' failures cannot revoke. The God who
saw Tamar weeping in the streets, who witnessed
Dinah's violation, who watched daughters in every
generation cry out for a mother who could not
come, that God has not looked away from any of
His daughters. We are held by a Heavenly Father
whose love does not fail, whose presence does not
waver, and whose care restores what was broken.
And where human mothering has fallen short, His
divine love remains whole, constant, and enough.

V

The Work That Remains
For Us All

11

A Call to Action

The Shift

Something is changing in the Black community. Younger generations of Black women are speaking openly about topics that their mothers and grandmothers were taught to bury. Previous generations were socialized to endure, demonstrate strength through silence, and honor family loyalty above personal well-being. But a new generation is reflecting on the notion that being strong includes saying, "No". Black daughters are beginning to understand that honoring yourself is not the same as dishonoring your elders, and sometimes healing requires distance. This shift is not happening in isolation. It is unfolding across social media platforms, in support groups, and during private conversations between friends who are finally admitting the pain their mothers caused. It is showing up in the rising number of Black women seeking mental health support, in the growing acceptance of therapy within the Black community, and in the willingness to name intergenerational trauma rather than perpetuate it.[1]

This shift is not without tension. Older generations often perceive younger women's boundary-setting as disrespect. Some older women view going to therapy as a weakness or taboo and perceive a daughter's willingness to detach as abandonment of cultural values. The generational divide is real, and it reflects fundamentally different understandings of what it means to be a Black woman, a Black daughter, and a Black mother. Yet this study revealed something remarkable. The Sagacious Seventeen are not rejecting Black culture. They are refusing to accept the parts of it that perpetuate harm. The daughters are not dishonoring their mothers by detaching. Rather, they are doing what is necessary so they can heal, break cycles, and mother differently if they are, or choose to become, mothers themselves. This is not rebellion. This is restoration. The cultural shift happening among younger Black women is not solely about individual healing. It is about collective transformation.

This chapter is a call to action. Not just for daughters, but for mothers, therapists, community leaders, and the church. The findings of this study are not merely descriptive. They are diagnostic. They reveal a public health crisis within Black families that has been ignored, minimized, or spiritually bypassed for far too long. The findings also point toward solutions. There are concrete, actionable steps that can be taken at every level to address the mother wound, support healing, and interrupt cycles of intergenerational trauma. Black daughters are asking for something different. They need acknowledgement, support, and change. So, this chapter is for them, and all of us who have a role to play in making that change possible.

For Daughters: Healing Is Your Responsibility, Not Hers

What the research shows is something you need to hear: You are not alone, you are not wrong, and your pain is valid.

One of the most aching realizations for many daughters is that their mothers may never apologize for the harm they caused. Waiting for your mother to begin your healing will keep you stuck. The daughters in this study did not wait for their mothers to validate their pain. They took responsibility for their own healing. The Sagacious Seventeen were actively engaged in therapy. Several were reading books on trauma, practicing self-compassion, and learning to identify and challenge the internalized beliefs that told them they were unworthy of love. The Sagacious Seventeen are doing the hard work of confronting the mother wound because they refused to spend the rest of their lives defined by it. You can do the same. Healing does not require your mother's participation. It requires your commitment. It may be one of the most loving things you ever do, not only for yourself, but for the generations that come after you.

You Are Not Responsible for Breaking the Cycle Alone

Many daughters expressed a deep motivation to "break the cycle" of intergenerational trauma. This desire is honorable. Simultaneously, it is important to acknowledge that breaking cycles is hard work, and you do not have to do it alone. Seek out community. Find other Black women who understand, whether through support groups, online communities, or friendships with women who have similar experiences. Connection is essential (and a part of our heritage). Isolation intensifies shame. Community dispels it.

Additionally, seek professional support. Therapy, especially with a Black woman therapist who understands the cultural dynamics at play, can be transformative. If financial barriers make therapy inaccessible, look into community mental health centers, sliding scale providers, or faith-based counseling services. Also, lean into your faith. God is not your mother. His love is not conditional. His care is not inconsistent. His presence is not absent. The spirit of adoption the Bible speaks of is real, and it is for you.[2] Let Him be a Father — and the Mother — that your earthly mother could not be.

For Mothers: A Mirror and an Invitation

If you are a Black mother whose daughter has detached from you, or whose relationship with you is strained, this may have brought up defensiveness, hurt, or anger. That is understandable. You must hear this, though. The daughters in this study are speaking not just for themselves, but for a generation of Black women who have been wounded by the very people who were supposed to protect them.

You Are a Wounded Daughter, Too

You are not a villain. You might be a wounded daughter yourself. The findings of this study made it clear that many of the Sagacious Seventeen's mothers were women who had been shaped by their own unhealed trauma and their own strained relationships with their mothers. You may have become a mother before you had the chance to heal from your own childhood. It is possible that you parented from a place of exhaustion, overstimulation, or unresolved pain. You probably did the best you could with what you had. Understanding why you struggled does not erase the impact of your struggles on your daughter. It does mean, though, that healing is possible for you, too. You do not have to remain trapped in patterns you inherited. You can choose differently, even now.

What Your Daughter Needs You to Hear

Your daughter did not detach from you to hurt you. She detached to protect herself. It likely came after years of hoping things would change, trying to make the relationship work, and adjusting herself to fit what she thought you needed from her. When she finally stepped back, it was not because she stopped loving you. Staying close was costing her too much. If your daughter has tried to talk to you about the harm she experienced, and you responded with defensiveness, dismissal, or blame, she learned that it was not safe to be honest with you. If she has asked for an apology and you deflected, minimized, or turned the conversation back to your own pain, she learned that her feelings do not matter as much as yours. If she has set boundaries and you violated them — showing up unannounced, calling repeatedly when she asked for space, using guilt or manipulation to pull her back in — she learned that you do not respect her autonomy. These responses are understandable. It is painful to be told that you hurt someone you love, especially when you were doing the best you could. If you want any hope of repairing the relationship, you must get comfortable with sitting in that discomfort. You have to be willing to listen without defending, acknowledge harm without justifying, and take responsibility without expecting your daughter to comfort you through your guilt. Most importantly, you will need to forgive yourself, and possibly your own mother if she gave you less than what you deserved.

Accountability Is Not Condemnation

Taking accountability does not mean you are a terrible person. It means you are a human being who made mistakes and who is willing to own them. Sometimes mothers cause the most pain when they refuse to acknowledge any harm at all. Accountability looks like this:

"I hear you saying that my words hurt you. I apologize."

"I did not show up for you the way you needed. That was not okay."

"I was dealing with my own pain, and I let it spill onto you. You did not deserve that."

"I want to understand what you went through. Will you help me see it from your perspective?"

Accountability does not look like:

"Well, you hurt me, too."

"I did the best I could. You need to get over it."

"You are being too sensitive."

"Other people had it worse, and they turned out fine."

Your daughter does not need you to be perfect. She needs you to be honest. She needs you to show her that you care.

You Can Break the Cycle Too

If you recognize yourself in the patterns described in this book, it is not too late to change. The daughters in this study expressed a desire not only for their own healing, but for their mothers' healing as well. Several acknowledged that their mothers were products of their own painful circumstances, wishing they had access to the support they needed to parent differently. You can get that support now. Therapy is for mothers who are carrying trauma they never processed, struggling with mental health issues they were taught to hide, and realizing that the way they were parented is not the way they want to be remembered. Black maternal mental health support is growing, and there are resources available. Community-based programs, faith-based counseling, and peer support groups can all provide space for you to process your own pain and develop the emotional tools you may never have been given. You do not have to do this alone. There is a chance for you to not remain stuck in patterns that are hurting both you and your daughter.

The Invitation

Here is the invitation. Be brave enough to look in the mirror. Be humble enough to listen. Be committed enough to change. Even if reconciliation never happens, you can still heal and interrupt the cycle. If your daughter does extend an opportunity for repair, willing to try again under new terms, do not waste it! Show up differently. Give genuine apologies. Respect her boundaries. Prove through your actions, not just your words, that you are capable of change. That is how you begin to move forward.

For Therapists: Cultural Competence in Treating Black Women

Mental health professionals have a critical role to play in supporting Black women who are navigating maternal detachment. To be effective, therapists must move beyond generic approaches to treatment and embrace cultural competence that is specific, informed, and responsive to the unique experiences of Black women.

Why Cultural Competence Matters

Research consistently demonstrates that Black women prefer — and benefit from — working with therapists who understand their cultural context.[3]

When asked about their preferences for mental health providers, Black women in multiple studies emphasized the importance of working with someone who looks like them, and who does not require them to explain the basics of what it means to be a Black woman in the United States.[4] Additionally, mistrust and a lack of cultural competency and empathy were identified as the main reasons Black women either avoided therapy altogether or discontinued treatment prematurely.[5] This is not about preference for the sake of comfort. It is about effectiveness. When Black women work with therapists who lack cultural awareness, they often experience microaggressions, stereotyping, and dismissal of their concerns. These misfortunes reproduce the very harm they are seeking therapy to heal from. Conversely, culturally adapted treatments have been shown to improve therapeutic outcomes, strengthen the therapeutic alliance, and increase client engagement and retention.[6] For Black women dealing with maternal detachment, cultural competence is not optional. The decision to detach is already laden with cultural and spiritual weight. Therapists who pathologize that decision and do not acknowledge a Black woman's family system or culture will do more harm than good.[7]

What Cultural Competence Looks Like in Practice

Cultural competence begins with humility. It requires therapists to acknowledge what they do not know and to approach each client as the expert on her own experience. It involves understanding the historical and systemic forces that shape Black women's lives and recognizing how those forces contribute to intergenerational trauma.

Specific competencies include:

Understanding the Black family context. Black families are not monolithic, but they often operate with cultural values that differ from White, middle-class norms. Collectivism, extended kin networks, and respect for elders are central to many Black families. Therapists must understand these dynamics without romanticizing them or using them to pressure clients to remain in harmful relationships.

Recognizing gendered racial socialization. Countless Black women are socialized to be strong, self-reliant, and protective of their families and communities. This socialization serves survival purposes but also contributes to emotional suppression, difficulty asking for help, and tolerance of mistreatment. Therapists should explore how these messages have shaped clients' identities and relationships.[8]

Addressing intergenerational trauma. The concept of intergenerational trauma is essential for understanding maternal detachment among Black daughters. Therapists should help clients explore how their mothers' behaviors may have been shaped by unresolved trauma, while also holding space for clients' pain and validating their need for boundaries.

Validating detachment as a protective strategy. Therapists must resist the urge to push for reconciliation as the ultimate goal of therapy. For some Black daughters, detachment is the healthiest choice. Therapists should support that decision, explore its impact, and help clients navigate the complex emotions that accompany it, without suggesting that the goal is to repair the relationship.

The Cost of Incompetence

When therapists fail to demonstrate cultural competence, Black women are harmed. They may feel misunderstood, dismissed, or re-traumatized. They may disengage from therapy altogether, reinforcing the belief that mental health care is "not for them." They may miss out on the healing that is possible when they work with providers who truly see them, understand them, and honor their experiences. The daughters in this study emphasized that therapy was essential to their healing. However, the reality is that not all therapy is created equal. Black women deserve therapists who are equipped to meet them where they are, understand the cultural waters they are navigating, and support their healing without adding to their burden.

For the Community: Maternal Mental Health and Trauma Recovery

Strained mother-daughter relationships within the Black community are not merely an individual or familial issue. They are communal ones. Addressing it requires community-level interventions that support maternal mental health, facilitate trauma recovery, and create systems of care that Black mothers and daughters desperately need.[9]

The Crisis of Black Maternal Mental Health

Black mothers experience maternal mental health conditions at alarmingly high rates. Despite these elevated risks, Black mothers are half as likely to receive treatment for maternal mental health conditions compared to White women.[10] The barriers are multifaceted: stigma around mental illness within the Black community, mistrust of healthcare systems due to histories of medical racism, lack of access to culturally competent providers, economic constraints, and systemic inequities that make it difficult for Black mothers to prioritize their own mental health when they are simply trying to survive.[11] And, as this study shows, daughters bear the consequences when mothers are not supported.

What Communities Can Do

Addressing Black maternal mental health requires coordinated, community-based efforts that meet mothers where they are and provide support that is accessible, affordable, and culturally resonant. The following strategies have been identified by researchers and practitioners as essential pathways toward equitable maternal mental health care.[12]

Invest in maternal mental health programs. Community-based organizations should develop and expand programs specifically designed to support Black mothers' mental health. This includes prenatal and postpartum mental health screening, peer support groups led by Black women who have lived experience, parenting classes that teach emotional regulation and trauma-informed parenting, and access to mental health professionals who specialize in maternal mental health.

Create trauma recovery programs. Intergenerational trauma is a defining feature of many Black families' experiences, and it requires intentional intervention. Trauma recovery programs should integrate trauma-informed care principles with sociocultural attuned approaches that acknowledge the historical, racial, and systemic factors contributing to Black women's trauma. Programs should be designed not just for individuals but for the healing of the entire family, creating opportunities for mothers and daughters to process intergenerational patterns together when both parties are willing and ready.

Facilitate intergenerational dialogue. One of the tensions revealed in this study is the generational divide in how detachment is perceived. Older generations often view it as disrespect, while younger generations see it as self-care. Community-based initiatives that bring multiple generations of Black women together — through facilitated dialogue, storytelling circles, or healing retreats — can help bridge this divide. These spaces should be led by Black women facilitators who understand the cultural dynamics and can hold space for differing perspectives while prioritizing safety and respect.

Partner with faith communities. Given the central role of the Black church in many Black communities, partnerships between mental health providers and faith leaders are essential. Churches can serve as sites for mental health education, screening, and support. They can reduce stigma by normalizing conversations about mental health from the pulpit and in small groups and connect mothers to professional resources while also offering spiritual support. This collaboration should be reciprocal, with mental health professionals offering training to clergy and church leaders on recognizing signs of maternal mental health distress and making appropriate referrals.

Center Black women's voices in program development. Too often, programs designed to support Black mothers are created without meaningful input from the very women they aim to serve. Community-based initiatives must be co-designed with Black mothers, informed by their lived experiences, and responsive to their stated needs. This requires humility from professionals and organizations, a willingness to share power, and a commitment to ensuring that Black women are not just recipients of services but architects of the solutions.

For the Church: Discipleship, Parenting, and Spiritual Warfare

The church has always been a cornerstone of the Black community, a place of worship, refuge, resistance, and hope. When it comes to Black mother-daughter relationships, it must evolve to address the spiritual, relational, and identity crisis facing Black mothers and daughters:

The first area of change is parenting education. The church invests considerable resources in preparing people for marriage. But what happens after the wedding, when children come, and parents find themselves replicating the very patterns they swore they would not repeat? How does a single mother access the same pastoral support that married couples receive? God is a God of generations, and the church has both the opportunity and the responsibility to equip parents—married and single, new and seasoned—with practical tools for raising children well. This means parenting classes that teach emotional regulation, healthy communication, conflict resolution, and biblical principles for nurturing children at every developmental stage. It means creating space for mothers to be honest about their struggles without fear of judgment. Many mothers are parenting from unhealed wounds, repeating inherited patterns, not because they do not love their children, but because no one ever showed them another way. The church can interrupt those cycles.

The second area is discipleship for both mothers and daughters. Discipleship programs should support mothers and daughters in navigating forgiveness, setting appropriate boundaries, pursuing emotional healing, and understanding their identity in Christ. For many daughters, their mothers' treatment has become conflated with God's character. The church must help them untangle that confusion, offering a clear and compassionate portrait of a Heavenly Father whose love bears no resemblance to the harm they experienced. For mothers, discipleship means accountability, the kind that does not shame but does not enable her behavior, either. It means creating relationships with spiritual leaders and mentors who know them well enough to speak truth into their lives.

The third area is the most urgent: the church must stop weaponizing Scripture. When daughters come forward with experiences of harm, the response cannot be to quote Exodus 20:12 and send them back to what broke them. It must be pastoral care: genuine listening, validation of pain, and honest engagement with the counsel of the Holy Spirit, which holds mothers accountable just as clearly as it calls daughters to honor. Jesus did not dismiss the suffering of the wounded. He did not bypass their pain with theological correctness. He tended to their needs with Scripture and love.

Finally, the church is uniquely positioned to address the spiritual dimension of the mother wound in ways no other institution can. Women need to understand that the rift between mothers and daughters is not solely relational and psychological. It is spiritual, a manifestation of a larger assault on womanhood, identity, and generational continuity. Teaching congregants to recognize this spiritual dimension does not mean demonizing mothers. It means equipping daughters to understand the forces at work, to engage in spiritual warfare with clarity, and to pursue healing that addresses the soul as well as the psyche. If secular therapists can accompany daughters on their journeys toward healing, how much more might the church be equipped to hold this work with spiritual care, communal accountability, and compassion? As the Body of Christ, the church faces a choice: It can continue to reinforce the patterns that have wounded daughters across generations, or it can become a conduit of liberation, leading the work of setting the captives free.

A Change on the Horizon

What is unfolding among younger Black women is a reclamation of their humanity. It is a refusal to accept that strength must mean silence, that honor requires enduring harm, or that love demands self-sacrifice to the point of self-erasure. It is a declaration that they — like all of God's daughters — are worthy of love, peace, and the freedom to become who they were created to be. That declaration extends beyond the daughters themselves. It is also for their mothers, who are also daughters carrying wounds of their own. It is for their families and communities, which flourish when women are whole. It is for the church, which most faithfully reflects God's heart when it stands with the wounded and the weary. And it is for the generations yet to come, with the hope that future Black daughters may grow up never having to heal from the hands that were meant to hold them.

Encouragement from the Sagacious Seventeen

Before I closed each interview with the Sagacious Seventeen, I asked one final question: What would you say to other Black women walking a similar path of being detached from their mom? Their responses are offerings of truth, survival, and hard-earned wisdom. They speak from places of grief, courage, faith, and healing. Some words carry a warning. Others extend comfort. Many reflect the tension of loving a mother while choosing distance from her. If you are walking this journey, these words are offered to you.

Shandra

"If you need to cut your mother off, that's okay. Take the time to do the work on yourself, to strengthen yourself, to process your feelings and grieve, honestly. One thing that one of my therapists had me do was write a letter to my mom about the disappointments, the heartbreaks, and, you know, what type of mother I needed that I didn't receive. I wrote the letter, I burnt the letter, and I let the ashes go.

Working with a therapist who understands you and can help you on this journey is important as well. And then surrounding yourself with people who support you, who get you. So don't hide behind that shield of shame. Talk to people. You're not alone. You did nothing wrong. And to find something in life that brings you joy, even if it's something little, and hold on to that thing and foster it and feed it and let it grow within you because that will be your safe space when you're feeling triggered, or you're feeling overwhelmed."

Corrine

"Protect yourself first."

Diana

"Protect your peace. Protect your energy. Protect your mind. Stop looking for people to rescue you, because they're not."

Jen

"Choose yourself."

Charity

"What's important is making sure that women are taking the time to have all of these experiences, heal, travel, and get to know themselves, before introducing a child into a mess."

Lisa

"Put yourself first. Put yourself first. Do whatever you can to think about yourself. Don't feel obligated. Don't feel obligated to be emotionally supportive or available to someone who isn't reciprocating."

Destiny

"Don't feel guilty for choosing yourself. It is okay to put yourself first… It's going to be a rough journey. I'm not going to sit here and make you feel like it's easy peasy lemon squeezy because it's not. But remember your purpose, and whatever you feel is still standing in your way from getting there, remove it. Whether that's your momma, daddy, sister, brother, cousin, uncle, nephew, niece, child... move it out of your way to get to where you're going."

Nia

"Love your mother. Love her how you need to love her so that you can love yourself. Because it took me a while to love myself. Because I've always viewed myself through her lens."

Amina

"Acknowledge that it hurts because a lot of times we won't acknowledge that it hurts. So, start with acknowledging that it hurts. Honor and respect your mother's humanity. And do what you need to do to make yourself feel loved healthily."

Michelle

"If you did not have the mother you wanted, you will always have what you need, even if that looks like through chosen family. I would also challenge them to redefine normalcy. So, if that means changing your holiday traditions or, you know, whatever it looks like for you. Take autonomy over your life and redefine what your life looks like.

Hope

"Growth hurts."

Moesha

"It's the most liberating journey they will come across. It will help them to connect with themselves. It is also a journey towards self-love. It's a cleaning of the house, and it sets the bar for how you or another Black woman will allow herself to be loved by anyone.

While there could be a father wound, the mother wound goes deep, and we can only accept the love from someone as deeply as we love and see ourselves. So, by detaching from our mother, we make room to really get to know ourselves and not try to seek and find that love in anyone else, whether it's romantic, or if it's a job, or if it's identity. It was the best thing that happened to me, and hopefully it's the same for other women."

Joy

"There's light at the end of the tunnel. Figure out your story and own your own story and own your journey and what that looks like for you. Healing is possible. And the last thing I'll say is cliché because I'm a person of clichés… Take it one day at a time. Every day is not going to be a great day, and that's okay. Every day is not going to be your great day… Oh yeah, Black women, lean into that whatever brings you joy and brings a smile to you."

Brooklyn

"It's not you. It's not you. So don't blame yourself. Have grace with your mom. We don't know the lives that they lived before us or what their childhood was like, especially if they don't talk about it and feel like a lot of, I feel like a lot of Back parents don't talk about their childhood and what happened to them. Give them grace but also understand that you don't have to have a relationship with them just because that's your mom."

Jasmine

"You're loved, regardless of whether your mom is in your life. I'd say that it's not easy. Nobody wants to be detached from their parent. Your parent is supposed to be the primary person who loves you unconditionally, and those feelings are really complicated… And, I would say it doesn't matter how old you get. There's always that inner little girl in you that is going to want your mom, and that inner girl deserves to be loved and to have a safe relationship, and it's said that she didn't."

Jada

"Don't play the comparison game. Lean into who you are as an individual outside of anyone, anything, or any situation. Start to really learn who you are, and that's going to help you navigate this space so much easier."

Mya

"Take as much time as you need to process everything and also be mindful about who you talk to about it, simply because there's gonna be a lot of people that say that's your mom and you should do this and this and that.

Figuring out what you need for yourself is going to be the most important thing, whether it is a relationship with your mom, whether it's not, it's just really taking the time to process a lot of that emotion and the feelings because that is the hardest thing."

The Sagacious Seventeen have spoken. May their voices remind every daughter who reads them: you are not alone, your healing is possible, and this is not the end of your story.

A Letter to Black Daughters

Dear Black Daughter,

I want to begin by saying this plainly… I see you. You are not too much. You are not too sensitive. You are not inadequate. You are not unlovable.

This book began with a question about TV moms, but what I was really asking was something deeper. I wanted insight into what the Sagacious Seventeen needed but didn't receive from their mothers. For the ones who chose Clair Huxtable, they wanted a present mother who corrected without abuse, a figure they could look up to. Daughters who chose Aunt Viv desired the same, along with financial stability. And, for the ones who surprisingly said Tina Belcher, I learned that they wanted a mother who was intensely devoted and supportive, allowing her children to be spunky and whimsical.

Regardless of which TV mom they chose, what unified the daughters was that they longed for something from their mothers, someone who was not able or willing to provide whatever it was. You may feel the same way about your mother. If you do, I apologize that you got less than what you deserved. How your mother treated you does not define your worth. It does not make you damaged goods. And it most certainly does not have to shape your future. It is not easy, but you can do the work to ensure the cycle ends with you. I need you to heal. Our community needs you to heal. And the little Black girls who will soon come into the earth deserve a healed version of you. It's possible, but not within your own strength. I say this as a Black daughter who was wounded by her mother, and yet somehow managed to get to a place where I could worship the Lord while kneeling beside my mommy's casket, thanking Him for many reasons. For my own healing. For being able to forgive my mommy ten months before her death. For always being present when I felt abandoned. He did it for me, I know He can do it for you. You just have to let Him… let Him show you that He is nothing like your mother. Let His perfect, unconditional love heal you. Let Him touch your heart, to mend it back together. And through intimacy with Him, you will begin to understand that what happened to you is less than God's perfect will for you, but He is working it out for your good.

Wherever your journey leads next—toward reconciliation, continued distance, or something entirely new—I hope you walk forward knowing this:

You are worthy of love that does not wound. You always were and always will be.

With care,

Dr. Steele

Endnotes

Chapter 1

[1] Hoffner, C. A., & Bond, B. J. (2022). Parasocial Relationships, Social Media, & Well-Being. *Current Opinion in Psychology, 45*(1), 1–6. https://doi.org/10.1016/j.copsyc.2022.101306

[2] Cohen, J. (2001). Defining Identification: A Theoretical Look at the Identification of Audiences With Media Characters. *Mass Communication and Society, 4*(3), 245–264. https://doi.org/10.1207/s15327825mcs0403_01

[3] Brock, A. (2020). *Distributed Blackness: African American cybercultures.* NYU Press.

[4,5] McLeod, C. N. (2025). Black Twitter as "Master" Social Architects: Maintaining Online Community Boundaries Through the Production of Time and Place. *Social Media + Society, 11*(3). https://doi.org/10.1177/20563051251374500

[6,7] Collins, P. H. (2021). *Black feminist thought: Knowledge, consciousness, and the politics of empowerment* (3rd ed.)

[8-10] West, C. M. (2018). Mammy, Sapphire, Jezebel, and the bad girls of reality television: Media representations of Black women. In D. C. Allison (Ed.), *Black women's portrayals on reality television* (pp. 139-163). Lexington Books

[11] Germain, M. (Writer), & Lauten, C., Warner, M-J. (Directors). (1990). Off to See the Wretched In M. Carsey (Producer), *The Cosby Show.* New York, NY: JC Studios.

[12] McGhee, Z., Lirtzman, M. (Writers), & Richardson-Whitfield, S. (Director). (2017). Tick Tock In S. Rhimes (Producer), *Scandal.* Los Angeles, CA: Sunset Gower Studios.

[13] Fish, M. (Writer), & Raju, S. (Director). (2017). Something Borrowed In S. Rhimes (Producer), *Scandal.* Los Angeles, CA: Sunset Gower Studios.

[14] McGhee, Z., Lirtzman, M. (Writers), & Richardson-Whitfield, S. (Director). (2017). Tick Tock In S. Rhimes (Producer), *Scandal.* Los Angeles, CA: Sunset Gower Studios.

[15] Van Dusen, C., (Writer), & Bokelberg, O. (Director). (2013). YOLO In S. Rhimes (Producer), *Scandal.* Los Angeles, CA: Sunset Gower Studios.

[16-20] Steele, Imani S., "Unmothered: A Phenomenological Study of Black Daughters Who Are Detached From Their Black Mothers"

(2026). *Doctoral Dissertations and Projects*. 7891.
https://digitalcommons.liberty.edu/doctoral/7891

[21]Ahmed, S. (2025). Achieving data saturation: Evidence from recent
qualitative studies. *Qualitative Research Journal, 25*(1), 1-15.
https://doi.org/10.1108/QRJ-02-2024-0012

[22] Steele, Imani S., "Unmothered: A Phenomenological Study of Black
Daughters Who Are Detached From Their Black Mothers"
(2026). *Doctoral Dissertations and Projects*. 7891.
https://digitalcommons.liberty.edu/doctoral/7891

[23] Braun, V., & Clarke, V. (2006). Using thematic analysis in psychology.
Qualitative Research in Psychology, 3(2), 77-101.
https://doi.org/10.1191/1478088706qp063oa

[24]Alford, A. M. (2021). Doing daughtering: an exploration of adult daughters'
constructions of role portrayals in relation to mothers.
Communication Quarterly, 69(3), 215–237.
https://doi.org/10.1080/01463373.2021.1920442

[25] Bowen, M. (1978). *Family therapy in clinical practice*

[26]Bowen, M. (1978). *Family therapy in clinical practice*

Chapter 2

[1-3] Steele, Imani S., "Unmothered: A Phenomenological Study of Black
Daughters Who Are Detached From Their Black Mothers"
(2026). *Doctoral Dissertations and Projects*. 7891.
https://digitalcommons.liberty.edu/doctoral/7891

[4-5] McCollum, E. E. (1991). A scale to measure Bowen's concept of emotional
cutoff. *Contemporary Family Therapy, 13*(3), 247–254.
https://doi.org/10.1007/bf00891804

[6-8] Steele, Imani S., "Unmothered: A Phenomenological Study of Black
Daughters Who Are Detached From Their Black Mothers"
(2026). *Doctoral Dissertations and Projects*. 7891.
https://digitalcommons.liberty.edu/doctoral/7891

Chapter 3

[1] Jones-Rogers, S. (2019). *They were her property: White women as slave
owners in the American South*. Yale University Press.

[2-3] Cowling, C., Toledo Machado, M.H.P., Paton, D., & West, E. (Eds.).
(2020). Motherhood, Childlessness and the Care of Children in
Atlantic Slave Societies (1st ed.). Routledge.
https://doi.org/10.4324/9780429260186

[4] Hartman, S. (2016). The Belly of the World: A Note on Black Women's
Labors. *Souls, 18*(1), 166–173.
https://doi.org/10.1080/10999949.2016.1162596

[5] Collins, P. H. (2006). The meaning of motherhood in Black culture and Black mother/daughter relationships. *SAGE: A Scholarly Journal on Black Women, 4*(2), 3–10.

[6] Bryant, L. S., Leath, S., Billingsley, J., & Moseley, S. (2024). "She Has a Village": The Intergenerational Benefits of Social Support Networks for Black Mothers and Daughters. *Psychology of Women Quarterly, 48*(3), 390-410. https://doi.org/10.1177/03616843241233289

[7] Louise Wood, A. (2018). The Spectacle of Lynching: Rituals of White Supremacy in the Jim Crow South. *American Journal of Economics and Sociology, 77*(3-4), 757–788. https://doi.org/10.1111/ajes.12249

[8] Greene, B. (1990). Sturdy bridges: The role of African-American mothers in the socialization of African-American children. *Women & Therapy, 10*(1-2), 205–225. https://doi.org/10.1300/J015v10n01_18

[9] Davis Tribble, B. L., Allen, S. H., Hart, J. R., Francois, T. S., & Smith-Bynum, M. A. (2019). "No [Right] Way to Be a Black Woman": Exploring Gendered Racial Socialization Among Black Women. *Psychology of Women Quarterly, 43*(3), 381-397. https://doi.org/10.1177/0361684318825439 (Original work published 2019)

[10] Dazey, M. (2021). Rethinking respectability politics. *The British Journal of Sociology, 72*(3), 580–593. https://doi.org/10.1111/1468-4446.12810

[11] Leath, S., & Mims, L. (2023). A qualitative exploration of Black women's familial socialization on controlling images of Black womanhood and the internalization of respectability politics. *Journal of Family Studies, 29*(2), 774–791. https://doi.org/10.1080/13229400.2021.1987294

[12-13] Davis, S. M., & Jones, M. K. (2021). Black Women at War: A Comprehensive Framework for Research on the Strong Black Woman. *Women's Studies in Communication, 44*(3), 301–322. https://doi.org/10.1080/07491409.2020.1838020

[14-15] Kemper, E. W., Brown, M. J., Lane, W. G., Mackey, A. K., & Christensen, M. L. (2021). The War on Drugs affects children too: Racial inequities in pediatric populations. *American Journal of Bioethics, 21*(4), 4-18. https://doi.org/10.1080/15265161.2021.1891336

[16] Rosino, M. L., & Hughey, M. W. (2018). The War on Drugs, Racial Meanings, and Structural Racism: A Holistic and Reproductive

Approach. *American Journal of Economics and Sociology, 77*(3-4), 849–892. https://doi.org/10.1111/ajes.12228

[17-18] Kohler-Hausmann, J. (2015). Welfare Crises, Penal Solutions, and the Origins of the "Welfare Queen". *Journal of Urban History, 41*(5), 756-771. https://doi.org/10.1177/0096144215589942 (Original work published 2015)

[19] Rambert, O. (2021). The absent Black father: Race, the welfare-child support system, and the cyclical nature of fatherlessness. *UCLA L. Rev., 68*, 324.

[20-21] Bailey, M. (2021). *Misogynoir Transformed*. NYU Press.

Chapter 4

[1] Steele, Imani S., "Unmothered: A Phenomenological Study of Black Daughters Who Are Detached From Their Black Mothers" (2026). *Doctoral Dissertations and Projects*. 7891. https://digitalcommons.liberty.edu/doctoral/7891

[2] Rohmah, L., Purwanta, E., & Sugito,S. (2023). Why should children have secure attachments? Literature review of the importance of attachment in child development. *Advances in Social Science, Education and Humanities Research*, 44–55. https://doi.org/10.2991/978-2-38476-114-2_5

[3-11] Steele, Imani S., "Unmothered: A Phenomenological Study of Black Daughters Who Are Detached From Their Black Mothers" (2026). *Doctoral Dissertations and Projects*. 7891. https://digitalcommons.liberty.edu/doctoral/7891

[12] Sooki, Z., Shariati, M., Chaman, R., Khosravi, A., Effatpanah, M., & Keramat, A. (2016). The Role of Mother in Informing Girls About Puberty: A Meta-Analysis Study. *Nursing and midwifery studies, 5*(1), e30360. https://doi.org/10.17795/nmsjournal30360

[13] Rohmah, L., Purwanta, E., & Sugito,S. (2023). Why should children have secure attachments? Literature review of the importance of attachment in child development. *Advances in Social Science, Education and Humanities Research*, 44–55. https://doi.org/10.2991/978-2-38476-114-2_5

[14-17] Steele, Imani S., "Unmothered: A Phenomenological Study of Black Daughters Who Are Detached From Their Black Mothers" (2026). *Doctoral Dissertations and Projects*. 7891. https://digitalcommons.liberty.edu/doctoral/7891

[18] Garber, B. D. (2021). The dynamics of enmeshed family system ten years later: Family court and contemporary understanding of adultification, parentification, and infantilization. *J. Am. Acad. Matrimonial Law., 34*, 97.

[19-21] Steele, Imani S., "Unmothered: A Phenomenological Study of Black Daughters Who Are Detached From Their Black Mothers" (2026). *Doctoral Dissertations and Projects.* 7891. https://digitalcommons.liberty.edu/doctoral/7891

[22] Borchet, J., Lewandowska-Walter, A., & Rostowska, T. (2018). Performing developmental tasks in emerging adults with childhood parentification–insights from literature. *Current issues in personality psychology, 6*(3), 242-251.

[23-39] Steele, Imani S., "Unmothered: A Phenomenological Study of Black Daughters Who Are Detached From Their Black Mothers" (2026). *Doctoral Dissertations and Projects.* 7891. https://digitalcommons.liberty.edu/doctoral/7891

[40-41] Wagner, S. (2023, March 10). *What is the Mother Wound | Mother Wound Project.* Mother Wound Project. https://www.motherwoundproject.com/post/whatisthemotherwound

[42] Steele, Imani S., "Unmothered: A Phenomenological Study of Black Daughters Who Are Detached From Their Black Mothers" (2026). *Doctoral Dissertations and Projects.* 7891. https://digitalcommons.liberty.edu/doctoral/7891

[43-44] Wagner, S. (2023, March 10). *What is the Mother Wound | Mother Wound Project.* Mother Wound Project. https://www.motherwoundproject.com/post/whatisthemotherwound

[45-49] Steele, Imani S., "Unmothered: A Phenomenological Study of Black Daughters Who Are Detached From Their Black Mothers" (2026). *Doctoral Dissertations and Projects.* 7891. https://digitalcommons.liberty.edu/doctoral/7891

Chapter 5

[1-36] Steele, Imani S., "Unmothered: A Phenomenological Study of Black Daughters Who Are Detached From Their Black Mothers"

(2026). *Doctoral Dissertations and Projects*. 7891.
https://digitalcommons.liberty.edu/doctoral/7891

Chapter 6

[1-29] Steele, Imani S., "Unmothered: A Phenomenological Study of Black
Daughters Who Are Detached From Their Black Mothers"
(2026). *Doctoral Dissertations and Projects*. 7891.
https://digitalcommons.liberty.edu/doctoral/7891

Chapter 7

[1-3] Steele, Imani S., "Unmothered: A Phenomenological Study of Black
Daughters Who Are Detached From Their Black Mothers"
(2026). *Doctoral Dissertations and Projects*. 7891.
https://digitalcommons.liberty.edu/doctoral/7891

[4] Rnic, K., Dozois, D. J., & Martin, R. A. (2016). Cognitive Distortions,
Humor Styles, and Depression. *Europe's journal of
psychology*, *12*(3), 348–362.
https://doi.org/10.5964/ejop.v12i3.1118

[5-14] Steele, Imani S., "Unmothered: A Phenomenological Study of Black
Daughters Who Are Detached From Their Black Mothers"
(2026). *Doctoral Dissertations and Projects*. 7891.
https://digitalcommons.liberty.edu/doctoral/7891

[15] Ingle, M. (2018). Western Individualism and Psychotherapy: Exploring the
Edges of Ecological Being. *Journal of Humanistic Psychology*,
61(6), 002216781881718.
https://doi.org/10.1177/0022167818817181

[16-19] Steele, Imani S., "Unmothered: A Phenomenological Study of Black
Daughters Who Are Detached From Their Black Mothers"
(2026). *Doctoral Dissertations and Projects*. 7891.
https://digitalcommons.liberty.edu/doctoral/7891

Chapter 8

[1-23] Steele, Imani S., "Unmothered: A Phenomenological Study of Black
Daughters Who Are Detached From Their Black Mothers"
(2026). *Doctoral Dissertations and Projects*. 7891.
https://digitalcommons.liberty.edu/doctoral/7891

[24] World Bank. (2022, February 25). *The Social and Educational Consequences of Adolescent Childbearing - World Bank Gender Data Portal*. World Bank Gender Data Portal.

[25-27] Steele, Imani S., "Unmothered: A Phenomenological Study of Black Daughters Who Are Detached From Their Black Mothers" (2026). *Doctoral Dissertations and Projects*. 7891. https://digitalcommons.liberty.edu/doctoral/7891

Chapter 9

[1-10] Steele, Imani S., "Unmothered: A Phenomenological Study of Black Daughters Who Are Detached From Their Black Mothers" (2026). *Doctoral Dissertations and Projects*. 7891. https://digitalcommons.liberty.edu/doctoral/7891

[11] Dombrowski, S. C., Timmer, S. G., Blacker, D. M., & Urquiza, A. J. (2005). A positive behavioural intervention for toddlers: parent-child attunement therapy. *Child Abuse Review*, *14*(2), 132–151. https://doi.org/10.1002/car.888

[12-24] Steele, Imani S., "Unmothered: A Phenomenological Study of Black Daughters Who Are Detached From Their Black Mothers" (2026). *Doctoral Dissertations and Projects*. 7891. https://digitalcommons.liberty.edu/doctoral/7891

Chapter 10

[1-4] Gates Jr, H. L. (2022). *The Black church: This is our story; this is our song.* Penguin.

[5-8] Steele, Imani S., "Unmothered: A Phenomenological Study of Black Daughters Who Are Detached From Their Black Mothers" (2026). *Doctoral Dissertations and Projects*. 7891. https://digitalcommons.liberty.edu/doctoral/7891

[1] McCall, T., Foster, M., Tomlin, H., Adepoju, B., Bolton-Johnson, M., & Bellamy, C. D. (2025). "I think we're on a cusp of some change:" coping and support for mental wellness among Black American women. *Frontiers in psychology, 15*, 1469950. https://doi.org/10.3389/fpsyg.2024.1469950

[2] Romans 8:15-16 (*Amplified Bible*, 1965/2015)

[3-4] Williams, S. L., Lewis, J. A., Moody, C. T., & Consolvo, C. (2023). Black women, therapists of color, and psychological services: A systematic review. *Journal of Black Psychology, 49*(1), 3-39. https://doi.org/10.1177/00957984221102862

[5-7] Hall, G. C. N., Ibaraki, A. Y., Huang, E. R., Marti, C. N., & Stice, E. (2016). A meta-analysis of cultural adaptations of psychological interventions. *Behavior Therapy, 47*(6), 993-1014. https://doi.org/10.1016/j.beth.2016.09.005

[8] Carter, R. T. (2007). Racism and psychological and emotional injury: Recognizing and assessing race-based traumatic stress. *The Counseling Psychologist, 35*(1), 13-105. https://doi.org/10.1177/0011000006292033

[9-10] Parker A. (2025). What You Can Do: A Qualitative Study on Black Maternal Mental Health and Equity. *Healthcare (Basel, Switzerland), 14*(1), 61. https://doi.org/10.3390/healthcare14010061

[11] Young, N. (2025). How Medical Mistrust Serves as a Barrier to Mental Health Treatment in the African American Community. *Journal of Social Behavioral and Health Sciences, 19*(1). https://doi.org/10.5590/jsbhs.2025.19.1725

[12] Fix, R. L. (2022). An evaluation of building our nation's daughters (BOND): improving black single mother–daughter relationships and well-being. *Journal of Child and Family Studies, 31*(1), 237-246.

Coming Next from Dr. Steele

Behind this research was the author's own story.

In her forthcoming memoir, Dr. Steele shares the deeply personal journey that inspired her research: the love, conflict, loss, faith, identity, and healing that shaped her understanding of what it means to be "unmothered." It is a story of rupture and restoration, grief and growth, and the painful beauty of becoming whole. Dr. Steele takes you on the journey of how she and her mother both became wounded daughters, who eventually reconciled shortly before her mom's passing.

Some stories end before they are finished. This one finished just in time.

Turn the page for a first look.

Introduction

Sometimes I feel like a motherless child

Sometimes I feel like a motherless child

Sometimes I feel like a motherless child

A long way from home

A long way from home

September 2024
Imani
The air was warm with the crisp clarity of September. It was the kind of day that teased the edge of summer's farewell and fall's arrival. The sunlight beamed through the sanctuary's windows, shining on the congregation who swayed gently, their voices rising and falling like a soft tide as they joined the worship team in a medley of praise. The worship leader, a figure of grace and gratitude, let out a sound that seamlessly wove through the keyboard's chords like a golden thread. It was a song of reverence, the kind that drew hearts toward heaven and left souls completely surrendered to God. For me, though, it was the equivalent of a screeching sound that provoked my soul as if someone was scraping their fingernails on a chalkboard. I managed to avoid the song for almost two-and-a-half years, but at this point, there is no escaping it. I cannot run from this.

Simone.

My middle name, the name I call myself when I need to
get my ish together.

You are going to have to sit with your feelings.

As someone who tends to disassociate, this was a
challenge, but I could not escape reality when The Truth
was present. I observed the rest of the church relishing in a
sacred moment where time was standing still.

Girrlll, you are about to break.

I knew the moment was coming, and I could not stop it.

*Take deep breaths so you do not have a panic attack…. Breathe.
You are not ready for them to see you like this.*

For most of the church, this point of worship was a divine
moment in which time stood still, while, to me, the
familiar chords of the song, "Praise is What I Do," were
like an arrow, sharp and unrelenting, bringing me back to a
memory that never fades. As others were positioning
themselves to worship, I chose to be in a posture of pain.
The sanctuary's light appeared to be so warm and radiant
to all, but for me, it was exposing the mother wound that
remained. The thorn in my side that will never go away.

I got into the fetal position on the floor and asked God the
million-dollar question with tears rolling down my face,

"Why did you take her from me?"

He responded, with such sovereignty, ***"So you both could
be at peace."***

Welp. What do I say to that? Nothing.

After mustering up the strength to seat myself in a chair, I placed my head on my best friend's shoulder, who had been with me through it all, and I could not help but think about that rainy day in May.

May 27, 2022
Imani
The rain fell with a steady rhythm. It was a May morning where spring's typical warmth was shrouded in a cool mist. The vibrant greens of the season were dulled by a curtain of gray resembling the mourning that was taking place. I listened to the rain while lying awake in bed for a brief moment. I stayed up too late to finish my tribute.

This is not the day to be late, Simone.

I did not give myself a chance to ease into the day after waking up early. I never give myself a chance to ease into the day. Hopping out of bed like an Energizer Bunny, a manifestation of a dysregulated nervous system, I grabbed my hair products, the ones my mommy never got to use. I walked quietly downstairs to Grandma's living room, a space that brought back wonderful childhood memories. I looked at the brown couch, stitched with a retro design, that was a place of comfort to all who sat on it. Sometimes people preferred to sleep on the couch rather than a bed. Thinking about previous holidays and family gatherings, I envisioned the faces of happy people who loved to be together, including my parents. I saw a younger version of myself that was content with being in the midst of her aunts, uncles, and cousins. I spent many family gatherings eating from divided paper plates while sitting on that brown couch, always allowing my sweet potatoes and mac n' cheese to be combined. However, it was time to snap back to reality.

After making my way to the kitchen sink, I began my wash-and-go hair routine. It was the only hairstyle I knew how to do by myself, so I savored the moment. Despite the day's upcoming events, I allowed myself to enjoy doing my hair. As the shampoo lathered, that coconut-heavy scent filled the kitchen. It was rich and sweet, almost like the smell that lingered in the air when my mom used to wash my hair in our kitchen on Saturday nights. The shampoo emulsified in my hair, creating a sensation that soothed me. The conditioner created a slip, like a buttery, tropical smell, mixing that created a soft flip to detangle my curls, which put me at ease.

Thank you, God. I could use some ease.

Now it was time for the fun part. It is fascinating to watch a Black woman's hair being styled in its curly state. I take my time to watch the curls form after lathering the gel through small sections, from the root of the hair to the end of the strand, so it will create a cast around the cuticle. That's the key to getting a defined curl for a wash-and-go that you want to last.

Take your time styling, girl, because you are going to be pissed if it gets frizzy.

This was not the day to have frizzy hair. I need something to be predictable today.

Silent prayers were spoken internally as I diffused my hair. I did not feel the need to say anything out loud to Him. I made my demands clear back in the Philadelphia airport. After my hair was dry, I looked in the mirror. Analyzing my reflection as if I did not know who it was looking at me.

Yeah, you look like Jenny. I went back upstairs.

"Good morning!" I said cheerfully to Grandma.

"Hey! Morning."

I could not read her. I wonder what she is thinking.

I headed back into the room.

"Good morning", I said to my best friend, Grace.

She was finishing up her makeup so she could do mine.

"Good morning!"

She does not ask me how I am doing because she knows better. We need friends like that, people who can discern when to speak and when to stay quiet. I sat in silence as she did my face, allowing myself to carefully feel the stroke of each makeup brush and the patting of the beauty blender. I looked in the mirror once Grace finished.

She did not contour the way she usually does.

"It is a daytime face, so you are not going to have as much dimension as you would like", she said in response to the dissatisfied look on my face.

I convinced her to contour my cheeks a bit more. I then put on a blush pink Calvin Klein pleated dress, complemented with taupe patent leather pumps. I looked in the mirror once I was dressed. I was feeling pretty and at peace, despite the heaviness I anticipated as each drop of rain became a tangible reminder of what I lost.

It was time to go. I sat in the passenger seat of Grandma's SUV while she was still inside the house. I needed a moment to myself. A moment to breathe. A moment to collect myself before stepping into what the day would demand of me. Soon, I would have to be composed. Graceful. A class act. That is my role within my mommy's family. As Grandma and I pulled off, I watched the streets of Columbus, Ohio pass by, the ones I knew my whole life. Streetlights, corner stores, and shotgun houses all stood quietly, unchanged. This was all familiar, yet everything was different. Each turn of the road brought me closer to a destination that I imagined taking since my early teens.

Well, here is the bridge I have been waiting to cross.

Two hours later, I sat in the clergy's section of the pulpit. Cristabel Clack's voice soothed my soul as she sang, "All my life you have been faithful. All my life you have been so, so good…" I spent months curating a playlist of songs that were meant to help me regulate. Israel & New Breed's version of "Goodness of God" was the first song that was played in my ear. It was the perfect time to put that playlist to use, so I had Grace be my personal DJ, allowing the music playing in my AirPods to put me at ease.

My father was sitting beside me. My covering. Between him and the music, I was cool, preparing to listen to whatever bull-crap my great-uncle Ronny was going to say in the mic. Nana was determined to have her baby brother speak, a battle I was not going to win. If she was going to stand ten toes down behind anyone, it was going to be him. He was my mommy and I's uncle by name only. His arrogance and condescending tone were off-putting to me, even as a child.

What could you possibly say about a niece you barely knew? You were not there for her. You thought you would be able to tame her addiction by allowing her to stay in your house. Yet less than twenty-four hours after you picked her up, you dropped her back off.

I was agitated by his performance. He was presenting himself as a loving, caring uncle. Then again, it was typical of him to grandstand when an opportunity presented itself, especially in the pulpit, so I should not have been surprised. This was on brand for him.

Where was this energy when you found out what Calvin did?

I found it telling that Ronny could only speak to how my mom was as a little girl and not as an adult. He did not know her. He did not care enough to know her. Thankfully, Aunt Richelle was the next one to speak. Someone who could actually speak well of the person we were all remembering. Next up was Uncle Jerome, my mom's youngest brother; you could hear the anger in his voice.

Who are you mad at?

I knew he felt robbed of time. Despite us reconciling yesterday, I knew our relationship would likely never be the same.

I leaned over to my dad and asked quietly, "Do you want to go separately or together?"

"Let's go together!"

It was our turn to stand at the podium in the pulpit. I stood, analyzing the faces of the people seated. My father began to speak. His ex-wife, my mommy's body, laying in a casket, three feet in front of us. Nicole, my older sister by way of my mother, mutually agreed that we wanted our dad to speak. Nana attempted to put up a good fight to stop it, but I did not back down.

"He was there for her when you were not, and he did the one thing that meant the most to her, looked after her daughters!", I boldly said to her one week prior as she was finalizing the program.

She was quiet. What could she say? She did not want to admit that I was right. She knew to tread lightly with me when it came to my dad. Not only because she did not want to deal with my fury, but she was also reminded that her ex-son-in-law was married to her daughter for sixteen years. He knew every secret her family worked hard to keep.

"I may not be able to tell her story better than she can, but I come a close second!"

I chuckled as my dad made it clear, in his own way, that no one knew my mom, or her story, as he did.

Okay, talk your stuff then, Dad!

That statement carried weight. It was not a comment. It was a declaration. As if he were saying, "Y'all (specifically Nana) are not going to act like I do not know how we got here!"

Where was there? The end of my mommy's life.

The handful of people, including Nana and Ronny, who looked offended by my dad's provocation were the same ones who should have been held accountable for what happened to my mommy.

To some, it might be odd to have an ex-husband speak at a homegoing service, but it was comforting to me. I needed to hear what my dad was saying. I needed a reminder of the love they shared. It was the first time I had heard someone honor their ex-spouse. Then, it hit me.

Wow, he still loves her.

When your parents get a divorce, it is easy to get stuck seeing them as adversaries. During this moment—the last time where I would be in the same room with both of my parents—I was grateful to be reminded that there were more good times than bad, as my dad explained. I had gratitude that, even now, my daddy could speak of my mommy with love.

He finished his remarks, and now it was my turn. I approached the microphone with the music still playing in my ear.

I always knew I would end up in a pulpit, but I did not think THIS would be the first time I am up here.

I looked at the faces in the pews. Some were confused about me being up there. I knew many did not know what was going to come out of my mouth. My dad stood behind me, lending his unconditional support. I took a deep breath while taking the AirPod out of my ear and said:

"To be frank, I struggled to determine what to say today. As much as I do not want to admit it, this unfortunate circumstance leaves me wondering how others, including many of you, perceive my grieving process. For me, my mother's passing is a complex, multi-layered experience full of contradictions and dualities that are prone to judgment. I would be lying if I told you that everything was sunshine and roses because it was not. It would also be false for me to say that everything was terrible because it was not.... I am sure you can imagine the dichotomy that I have faced since the beginning of March (the time when my mother told me about her sclerosis of the liver that she was diagnosed with 6 years prior).

Nevertheless, God is a Redeemer. My mother and I's relationship is a testament to His ability to restore. He is glorified. For the past ten months, my mother and I mutually invested in our relationship; we put in the work. We forgave each other. We healed. We laughed. We loved. I knew this day would come but never expected it to happen at this point in my life. I grieve for twelve-year-old and thirty-four-year-old Imani because there are moments in life where a daughter should have her mother."

I honored my mother in a way that was respectful, yet honest. I never sugarcoated my feelings about her, and I was not going to start then. I looked outward towards those listening and noticed certain faces in the crowd. Nana, my mother's biological mom, had a look of worry as she was afraid of being exposed. The tension between us was high, and that was nothing new. I was the daughter of her only daughter, her eldest child, whom she did not like. Grandma, my mother's bonus mom—the one who is a grandmother to me—was not moved by anything I said. She was one of the few people in the room who knew my mommy and I's story and wanted to ensure that I was okay. One of my aunts, my dad's sister, and Grace were surprised that I was being candid with the room while preparing to tussle with anyone if need be. Although I could not see his reactions, I felt the energy of my father behind me. He was a proud papa bear who had my back. My father knew, more than anyone else in the room, the hell she put me…well, us, though. Nevertheless, he was pleasantly surprised that I managed to honor my mother without fabricating the dynamics of our relationship. Regardless of how anyone felt, it was important for me to pay respect to my mother without invalidating my feelings.

About the Author

Dr. Imani S. Steele is a brand strategist and researcher dedicated to understanding the architecture of relationships. With a background in brand and marketing strategy, working for Fortune 500 companies, Dr. Steele built her career studying how people form meaning, attachment, and trust with the brands in their lives. She now applies that same curiosity and rigor to understanding the strained and non-existent dynamics between Black mothers and Black daughters. Her work is both scholarly and personal, as she is a Black daughter who has navigated the terrain of a strained maternal relationship herself.

Dr. Steele continues to apply her brand and marketing strategy expertise across industries. Through Steele Compass, she bridges together all of this work: research that centers Black daughters, brand and marketing strategy that helps businesses grow sustainably, and storytelling that bridges scholarship and lived experience.

Follow Dr. Steele on social media to keep up with her journey:

Instagram: @imani_steele_
TikTok: @imani_steele_
Threads: @imani_steele

Want to book Dr. Steele for an event? Send your inquiries to bookings@theartofstories.org

Stay Connected

At Steele Compass, we've created a space where the work continues, with resources designed for Black daughters navigating the mother wound, business owners wanting to grow their brands, and scholars in need of culturally competent research centering Black daughters.

Visit steelecompass.com to access:

- Free downloads and e-books
- Practical tools and frameworks
- The Steele Compass blog, where Dr. Steele goes deeper into the research, life as a business owner, her faith, and her everyday work of becoming.

A Place to Be, Then Become